Planking Techniques
for
Model Ship Building

by Donald Dressel

TAB Books

Division of McGraw-Hill

New York San Francisco Washington, D.C. Auckland Bogotá
Caracas Lisbon London Madrid Mexico City Milan
Montreal New Delhi San Juan Singapore
Sydney Tokyo Toronto

© 1988 by **TAB Books**.
TAB Books is a division of McGraw-Hill, Inc.

pbk   20 21 DOC/DOC 0

Library of Congress Cataloging-in-Publication Data

Dressel, Donald.
    Planking techniques for model ship builders.

    Includes index.
    1. Ship models. I. Title.
VM298.D7   1988   623.8'201   87-35675

ISBN 978-0-07-183239-7

                                                                            HT3
Cover photographs courtesy of William F. Parkinson
                                                                            2868

Acknowledgments

THIS BOOK IS BASED ON MATERIAL AND KNOWLedge gained over a period of fifteen years spent in building ship models by both me and many members of the Ship Modelers Association of Fullerton, California. There is no way I can name all of the individuals of the Ship Modelers Association who have assisted me in my modeling efforts from the beginning fifteen years ago to the present date.

A few modelers have greatly assisted me in the preparation of this book. To the following people go my special thanks: Henry Bridenbecker for permitting me to "pick his brain" in several interviews and to photograph all of his beautiful models; Ed Marple for permitting me to interview him, take pictures of his beautiful models, and permit me to use many of the photographs he took while building the H.M.S. *Conqueror;* Bob Saddoris for the information he supplied in interviews and the photographs of his beautiful models; and to the other modelers who allowed me to take pictures of their models to grace the pages of this book.

Contents

Introduction

THE ART OF SHIP MODELING HAS BEEN IN EXIStence since the time of the Egyptian civilization. The abilities of ship modelers have continually increased until some of the finest models the world has ever seen are being made today. That this is possible is a result both of current technology and the ability to obtain information. It is the spreading of this information that is the main concern of this book.

Since I have been involved with the Ship Modelers Association of Fullerton for a number of years, it has become apparent that there are many fine ship modelers who labor away at their craft without realizing that other people out there in the world do the same thing. There are also techniques of planking ships that vary in many different ways among modelers. Even an expert can sometimes learn from the novice modeler, since the novice might come up with a new and unique way of doing a certain procedure.

This book is written to inform all ship modelers—novice, intermediate, or master, kit or scratch—that there are different ways of planking ships, that there are a number of construction methods, and that there are other people out there who enjoy the same craft.

I would also state at the beginning that there is no such thing as a bad ship model. There are simply some ship models that are better than others. The proper procedures and methods employed in planking ship models will go a long way to improve your efforts to build a "museum-quality" ship model.

The construction of a planked ship model is not something that can be done in a short time. The additional effort and time taken in doing the work will ultimately improve the final product. The book will start out with the materials, then the hull skeleton structure, and finally the planking procedures, which are those that most closely follow the actual practice used when building the real thing.

The planking of ship models is also not something that can only be accomplished by the expert wood craftsman. This art is not beyond anyone who can build a model, provided he has the main requirement: patience. It helps if your interest extends beyond just seeing the finished product. A real interest in the methods of construction, if not present at the beginning of your efforts, will develop as you strive to improve your product.

The product does not require an elaborate workshop or an extensive line of tools. Power tools are not necessary, although they can make the job much easier for the modeler. The quality of material used for construction (wood, glues, etc.) is very important to the modeler.

In short, the information in this book will be of help to all levels of modelers. Over 40 years of ship modeling experience will be compiled through material gathered both from my experience and the experience of several modelers from the Ship Modelers Association. It is my hope that this information will help other modelers to "get started," improve the product, and complete the model.

1

Planking Materials and Tools

THE FIRST ITEM REQUIRED TO BUILD A WOODEN ship model is the wood. What type of wood should you use for each part of the model and what is the basic beginning to planking ship models? If you have started with a ship model kit, then you already have the wood. A first suggestion is that you consider substitution of some of the wooden material in the kit.

The definition of *kit* used in this book refers to both solid-hull and plank-on-bulkhead kits. *Plank-on-bulkhead kits* are those ship model kits which have a rib structure made up of a backbone or keel and frames or bulkheads (FIG. 1-1). *Solid-hull kits* are one solid piece of wood (FIG. 1-2).

Scratch builders must provide their own wood for construction of the model. The types of wood available, the cost, and how good the wood is for ship model construction are of prime importance.

The seasoning of the wood is also very important. The wood should be air-dried if possible for at least one or two years after you have purchased it to make sure it is dry and will not warp, split, change color, or do some other strange thing. This too cannot be stressed too strongly. You do not want to spend a year or more building a ship model only to see it warp out of shape or twist into a funny position. This is one reason that plywood is a good wood to use for frame construction of plank-on-bulkhead ships.

WOOD

Plywood is made up of several laminations of glued-together wood, with the grain running alternately horizontally and vertically by layer. It is available in 3 ply and 5 ply. *Ply* refers to the number of layers of wood. Plywood can be cut in any direction without worry about grain direction or loss of strength, drilled and nailed without worry about splitting or breaking, and fitted tightly to another part without fear of breaking.

The best type of plywood is *birch* ply, both medium and best quality. Other types of ply should not be used. Because of its ugly appearance, use plywood only where it cannot be seen in the finished product. This would be for the frames, keelsons, deck beams, etc. Plywood is relatively cheap compared to other woods best suited for ship models.

At the other extreme is *boxwood*, a very expensive and hard to find type of wood. Boxwood is very strong, close-grained, hard, and has a yellowish color. This is the wood that was used to construct most of the Admiralty models. It is an excellent wood for carving and for planking. This is one of the best woods for ship modeling.

Pear is another excellent wood for planking. Light brown in color with short fibers and a plain grain pattern, pear has a medium-hard quality, which is excellent for planking and carving. This wood is also relatively expensive, but gives a beautiful finish. You can try to find someone with a pear tree in your area who will give you a few good pieces after trimming. If you obtain pear wood this way, do not forget to season the wood properly before use.

One of the woods a lot of people think should be used for model construction is *oak*. This is the wood that was used to build the real ships. It is hard, with a light tan color, and is short-fibered. There are some aspects of this wood that are not that good, preventing it from being very suitable for model construction.

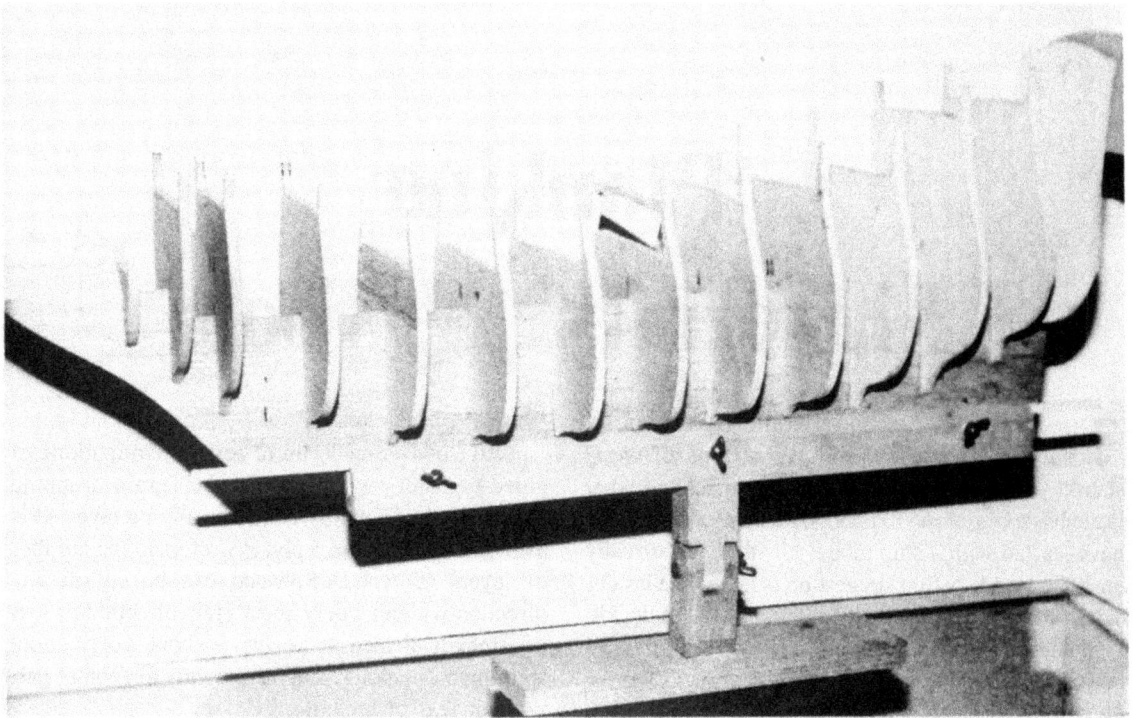

Fig. 1-1. An example of a typical plank-on-bulkhead structure supplied in kit form is my frame structure for the ship Fredrich Wilhelm zu Pferde.

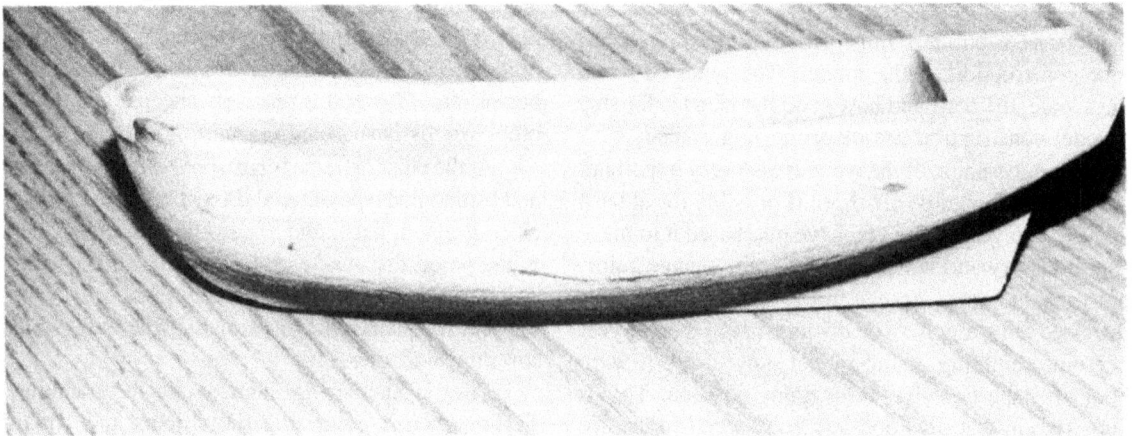

Fig. 1-2. An example of a typical solid-hull form from a kit model.

One of these is the rather large grain structure, which is very apparent if the model is to be left unpainted. It also has a coarse texture, which makes it difficult to work with. This wood is not recommended for ship modeling.

One wood that is supplied in ship kits is *spruce*. This wood is only good for underplanking and is rather difficult to work with. *Underplanking* is the method used in most kits where you in effect plank the hull twice. Since the first layer of planking is hidden by the second, it does not make much difference what wood is used, except in respect to the ease of working the wood. Spruce is a cheap wood and will make your model look cheap if you use it where it is visible.

Most kits do provide the modeler with a second layer of wood of better quality, such as *walnut*. Walnut is a hard, short-fibered, tough wood with a plain grain pattern. It comes in a variety of colors, from light to dark brown. It is an excellent wood for planking because it is easy to work and bend despite its hardness. Most ship model kits are furnished with walnut as the second layer of planking. Often this wood is not of the best quality. You can replace the kit wood, as suggested before. Walnut is expensive but not difficult to obtain.

Some kits contain *mahogany* as the planking wood. This wood is not very good for planking because it splinters very easily, but it is sometimes used since it is difficult to replace the color of this wood. It is a hard wood, sometimes red in color shading toward brown, with an obvious grain pattern.

Lime, linden, and *basswood* all refer to the same soft, white, tough, wood. It is excellent for planking ship models. Some kits come with this wood since it is relatively cheap. It is an excellent wood for planking purposes.

For the more exotic ship modeler, there are other woods that can be used for planking. These include *ebony*, a black wood, very hard and dense, which does not bend very easily and is difficult to use since it is very oily. Ebony must be cleaned with acetone just prior to gluing to the frame, first layer of planking, or solid hull. If it is not cleaned, it will not adhere to the model. If you are a modeler who loves wood and hates paint, this is the only way you can get black wood. It is difficult to use and hard to cut,

as well as being very expensive. It can be used in planking and will last without coming apart if treated right. I have used it on two of my models.

White holly is another fine wood to use for planking, the deck area being the prime choice since all decks on wooden ships were hollystoned to a white color. It is a stable, hard wood which is easily worked and bends easily. It is moderately priced to expensive, depending on where you live.

American cherry is an excellent wood for planking hulls. It has a very small grain and is a light reddish-brown. This wood is moderately priced and, if well seasoned, does not warp.

English sycamore is also an excellent wood for planking. The wood bends easily, does not splinter, and I found it fun to work with. It is a light tan to white color and is moderately priced. I used it on the lower portion of the hull of a clipper.

Red gum, or *satin walnut,* is a beautiful wood, which is fine grained and looks similar to pear but with a darker shade. It has no grain pattern and is a hard wood. The wood has been used on an Admiralty style model built by a member of the Ship Modelers Association of Fullerton with excellent results. Red gum is a moderately priced wood.

Split bamboo is the best material to use for making dowels. *Dowels* are the wooden equivalent of nails, which were used with brass and iron in the days of wooden ships to fasten down the planks. Bamboo is sometimes hard to find. Some modelers have used floor mats, brooms, and other items made from bamboo.

Poplar is another fine wood, which is sometimes overlooked by ship modelers. It is a light greenish color, is hard, does not split, and works very well. Henry Bridenbecker, an expert scratch ship-model builder, has used poplar a great deal and likes it very much. This wood is moderately priced.

White pine is an excellent wood for solid hulls. The wood carves very nicely and is not pitchy. It works very well when you are planking over the solid hull. Basswood and sugar pine are also excellent woods for this purpose. Most good solid-hull kits contain this type of wood hull.

Balsa wood is not suitable for wooden ship model construction. Although cheap, it is too porous, breaks easily, will not hold a nail, and looks very cheap. Weight is not of primary importance in static wooden ship model construction.

White peroba is another fine wood, which is so similar to boxwood that it is hard to tell the difference. It has all the same characteristics, but is also hard to get. The price for this wood is moderate. Also there is a beautiful *peroba rosa* if you can get it, which again has fine characteristics.

Whitebeam is a wood that is similar to pear with a fine grain. It has a light color, as the name suggests, and is moderately priced.

Pau marfin is a straw yellow wood, which is good for planking but tough to work with, since it is hard, like lemon wood, and has a tendency to splinter. The color is what is so good about this wood. It is also moderately priced.

All the woods mentioned have been used by ship modelers with excellent results. Cedar has been used also and turns out very nice, but is difficult to work with like pau marfin. Padauk has been used to plank an Egyptian ship because of its reddish-orange color. It is also a difficult wood to work with and has a tendency to turn darker with age, thus destroying the reddish-orange color which was the main reason for using the wood. Use care in selecting the wood to use.

Holly is really one of the best woods for planking if you can get it. Holly will take any strain and will look good after you stain it. Some of the woods indicated here will not stain well. If an Admiralty effect is your main desire, use boxwood, pear wood, or white peroba, if you can get them.

Some woods used in ship model construction, such as lemon wood, apple wood, Sitka spruce, lance wood or dagame, and other woods will not be covered in this text since they are used for steps other than planking.

Two other materials you can use for planking are bone and ivory. While difficult materials to work with, they can and have been used. Many of the prisoner-of-war models, built by prisoners during the Napoleonic War of the eighteenth century, were made of bone. Bone and ivory are difficult to obtain, and ivory is also expensive.

Alder is an excellent wood to use for planking, and looks very much like boxwood. Henry Briden-becker uses this wood for much of his planking, and says it works just like boxwood when well seasoned. Alder is not an expensive wood and can be obtained from most good lumberyards.

GLUE

The material to glue these woods together is also of importance. The best glue is the white aliphatic resin glue, such as Titebond Wood Glue. This glue gives you a few minutes to position the plank and can be cleaned up with a wet rag if you use too much glue. I have used this glue on all of my planked models and have not had it fail yet. It dries in about 10 minutes and becomes clear as it dries. A great amount of glue is not needed for a really strong bond.

Elmer's White Glue is another glue that can be used, but it is not as good as the aliphatic resin glues. Most of the professional woodworking glues are aliphatic resin glues, and Elmer does make such a glue.

Contact cement is good for putting copper on the hull over the planking, but is not much good for planking purposes because the glue sets too fast. The same can be said for the new instant glues such as Hot Stuff, Crazy Glue, and others.

The cyanoacrylate glues adhere to anything instantly, including your fingers if you are not careful. There are two kinds of this glue, the first of which requires a tight bond that is well fitted with no space or gaps in between. This glue bonds almost instantly. The second type is a little thicker and not as watery as the first and takes a little longer to dry. These glues are relatively new but have been used for several years by a number of modelers including myself with excellent results so far. When trying to glue metal to wood, this is the only glue outside of epoxy to use.

Two-part epoxy-resin glues give strong joints when gluing metal to wood or where stress is encountered when planking around the bow or stern area of a hull. These glues can be obtained from a number of manufacturers in a variety of setting times, from 5 minutes to many hours. Of all the glues available, my own choice for the job of planking the hull is the aliphatic resin glue noted first.

TOOLS

Before you can get on with the task at hand, you

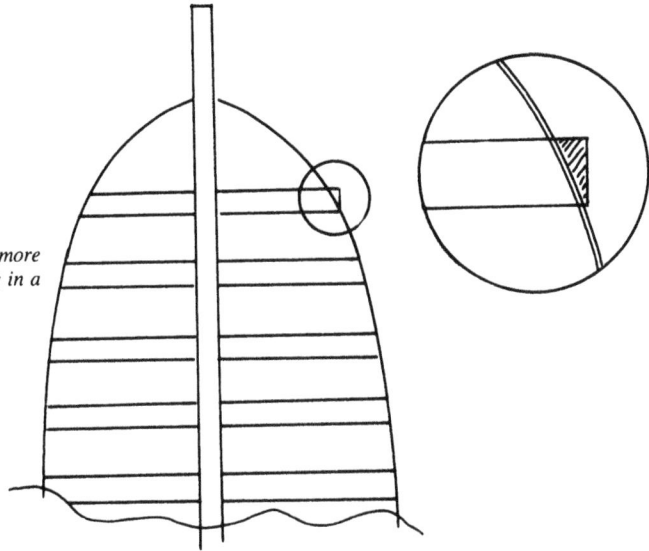

Fig. 1-3. Removing the edge of the bulkhead will enable more surface area to make contact with the plank, resulting in a smoother run of planking.

must obtain the proper tools to plank the model. By *tools* I am also referring to other items, such as jigs.

Both scratch builders and kit builders will be aided by having two large pieces of ¼-inch glass. Its main purpose is as a straightedge. When gluing the keel or backbone of the model together, you have to make sure it is absolutely straight. Glue the parts together and let them dry while positioned between the two pieces of glass and you will be assured of a straight keel. By *keel* I am also referring to the stem and sternpost and, in the case of the scratch builder, the deadwood.

Once dried (I like to wait overnight), you can remove the structure from between the glass and dowel it if desired. *Doweling* refers to the process of drilling a hole in the location for the wooden pin or dowel, dipping the dowel in a diluted solution of white glue, and driving the dowel into the hole like a nail. This process must be done quickly before the dowel starts to swell or it will not fit into the hole. Usually, you need to drill the hole one size larger than the dowel. (The making of dowels will be covered in Chapter 2.)

One primary tool for planking purposes is a set of proportional dividers. This tool allows you to find the width of your plank at different points along the plank. This tool can also be used as ordinary dividers to measure distances from the plans to the model or to enlarge or reduce the model from that shown

on the plans. (The use of this tool for planking will be explained further in Chapter 3.)

Sanding paper of various grades and sizes is required. Along with the sanding paper I find that a disk-type sander is very valuable. Sanding and shaping the planks, the frames, and almost all other parts of the model can be done by hand, but power tools sure speed up the work and make things a lot easier. At the same time, some parts of the model almost need to be done by hand with some care. *Beveling the frames*, which is the process of forming the edges of the bulkheads to the proper curve (FIG. 1-3), can best be done with a long flat tool (FIG. 1-4), which is basically a sanding block.

While on the subject of sanding, one tool which I feel is a basic tool is a powered hand-held drill/sander type machine such as the Dremel Moto tool. This tool is a little expensive and might not be for everyone, but I use it all the time for sanding, drilling, and carving with the various attachments that can be obtained for it. Even better is a dentist's drill, if you can find one that is not too expensive, as well as the other power tools of a similar nature.

Basic tools would include a small jeweler's hammer, which is used to drive the copper nails into the planks after a pilot hole is drilled. In order to drill the pilot hole, you need a small pin vise and a set of mini drills. These mini drills are numbers 60 to

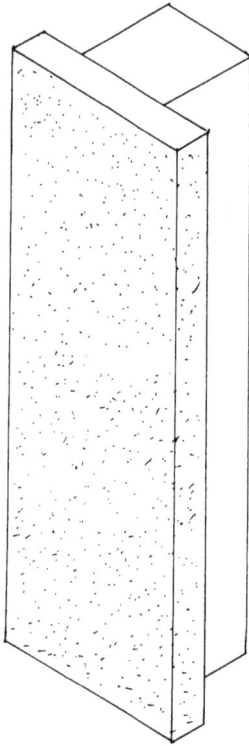

Fig. 1-4. A typical sanding block made with sandpaper glued onto two pieces of wood. It is best to use a long piece of wood to sand the ends of your bulkheads.

80, and are available in a set or can be purchased individually as desired. The mini drills also can be used with the Dremel Moto tool or its equal.

The X-ACTO type knife is another good tool to have in your shop for the planking process. This tool is used to cut and trim your planks. A fine-toothed Zona-type backsaw and miter box are also required for the end cuts of the planks.

You can also include a mini power saw, which will do all of the things the X-ACTO and backsaw will do and more. If you are scratch-building a model, the mini power saw will be invaluable for cutting your planks out of the wood stock. A number of mini power saws are available, such as the Dremel saw or its equal.

As an added item, you might consider the Unimat machine, which can do everything with the attachments for this unit. The Unimat is a saw,

jigsaw, planer, lathe, drill press, etc. It is rather an expensive item, but scratch builders will find this unit a must item.

I have used the Unimat and find it very accurate. A good modeler does not need these power tools, since he can build a fine model without them. They just make his work more enjoyable and faster. A jigsaw or jeweler's coping saw can do all of the work by hand at a fraction of the cost of the more expensive power tools.

Tapering the planks can be accomplished with a power disk sander or with a simple palm plane. I am mentioning all these tools because some modelers use one type of tool and other modelers do not.

The use of a good metal, six-inch scale with metric and English measurements is a must item for any modeler, even a kit builder. Curved areas can be difficult enough without complications resulting from improper measuring. Scale accuracy is a must for any ship modeler, be he kit or scratch.

A large quantity of thumb push-pins are invaluable for holding the planks against the frame while the glue is setting. Also useful are clothespins, large metal clamps, locking forceps, and any other clamping device both to hold the planks to the frames while the glue sets and to hold adjacent planks together. Some types of clamps are shown in FIG. 1-5.

Small files and rasps also can be of great help in getting at that tiny corner you cannot reach by any other method. These tools are used for both sanding and cleaning up. They have a special use by the modeler who is working with the solid-hull type of ship model, be it kit or scratch.

Chisels are also of great help and should be part of your tool collection. Include ⅛-inch, ⅜-inch, and 1-inch chisels.

Tweezers are sometimes needed even for just planking the ship, as well as a good pair of pliers. There is nothing worse than getting a push-pin set in the frame when the head of the pin comes off. The only way to remove the pin is with a pair of pliers. After using some push-pins for a model or two, you will find that a few of the push-pins have a tendency to lose their heads at just the wrong moment.

There are other items needed by the ship modeler to complete models, such as beeswax, but this item and others are not required for planking the ship.

One tool is of great assistance when planking your model, although it is not mandatory. This is the electric plank bender by Aeropiccola of Italy. There have been times when this tool saved my life while planking a ship in the bow area and stern area, two of the most difficult areas to plank. Again, this does not imply that this tool is essential, just that at times it can help you over a rough spot.

JIGS

You also can make a number of jigs to make your life a lot easier. The first and most obvious is the baseboard on which you will build your model. Most kits do at least indicate this first step. An improvement has been designed by Dick Roos, a member of the Ship Modelers Association. He built a baseboard with

an adjustable keel holder made out of aluminum. Bend two pieces of aluminum at 90 degrees, drill holes in both sides of each piece (FIG. 1-6), and bolt or screw the aluminum pieces to the baseboard with just enough room for the keel to fit between them. Make the fit snug, but not so tight that it binds. You will have to remove the model to handle it once in a while and you do not want to ruin your keel.

Make the baseboard out of a good piece of plywood that is flat and absolutely true. Do not try to skimp here because you may warp your keel, thus ruining your model.

Please check your keel to make sure it is flat and true, especially if you are building a kit model. If the keel, stem, and sternpost are not true, your model will come out crooked. If it is not true, wet the keel assembly and place it between the two pieces of glass mentioned earlier. Once it is true and flat, keep it

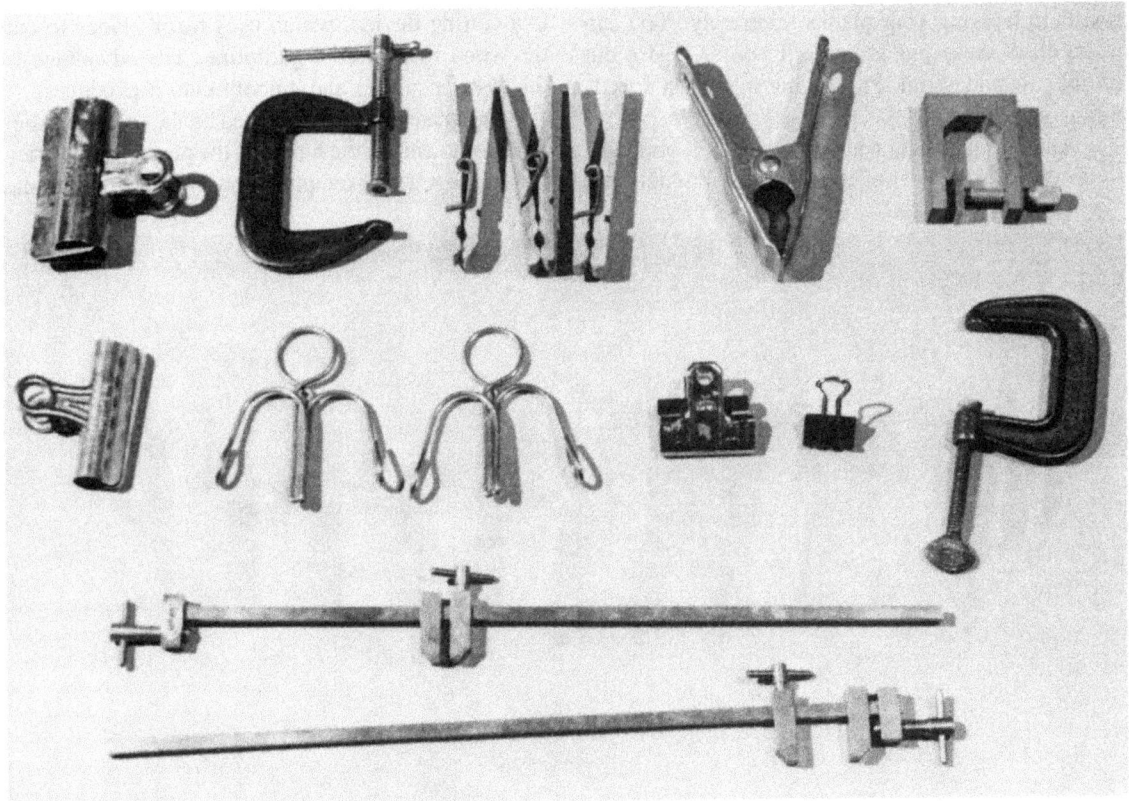

Fig. 1-5. Various kinds of clamps that are used to help you do your planking.

so by placing it into your keel holder on your baseboard and keeping it there.

Another jig that is important when planking ship models is shown in FIG. 1-7. This is simply a piece of wood that has been shaped to fit the curve of the bow with two clamps to hold down the wood planks. Soak the planks in ammonia water to make them easier to bend and then insert them into this form to dry. After they have dried, they will keep the bent form and will be much easier to install at the bow area.

Other versions of this form give the same result, and can be purchased if you so desire. One source is Scale Nautical Tools & Supplies. They have a plank-tapering jig, a plank-bending jig, and a framing clamp, all of which I have used with success. The framing clamp is to ensure the bulkheads and keel of a kit-built ship are squared to each other. The plank-bending jig is another version of the wooden jig with the added feature that it is adjustable to the curve of your own model. The plank-tapering jig assists in tapering your planks accurately. You can make all of these jigs at home if you so desire out of your own material. Purchasing them just speeds things up a little.

Another jig or tool which is essential if you want to dowel your model, as most scratch builders do,

is the drawplate, which can be hard to find and also expensive (FIG. 1-8). The only way I am aware to form your dowels to the proper size is by drawing them through the drawplate.

If you cannot find a drawplate, you can make one out of a piece of steel. Take a hardened piece of steel, such as an old, broken hacksaw blade, and drill holes in it with your saw. Drilling the holes might cause you to break some of your drills, but it is cheaper than buying your own drawplate. When making the dowel, draw the wood through the rough part of the hole with the jagged edges since this is where the cutting is done.

The precision miter tool used to cut wood at precise angles with great accuracy is also a good tool to acquire. There are several different versions of this same tool put out by various manufacturers. One of these is Scale Nautical Tools & Supply.

Some of the members of the Ship Modelers Association have made this tool themselves. The tool is a cutting device, which uses razor blades to cut the wood much like a guillotine. The advantage is the fast, accurate, and smooth cuts it produces.

Templates (FIG. 1-9) are used by the solid-hull ship modeler to ensure the hull is of the proper shape prior to planking. These templates must be made according

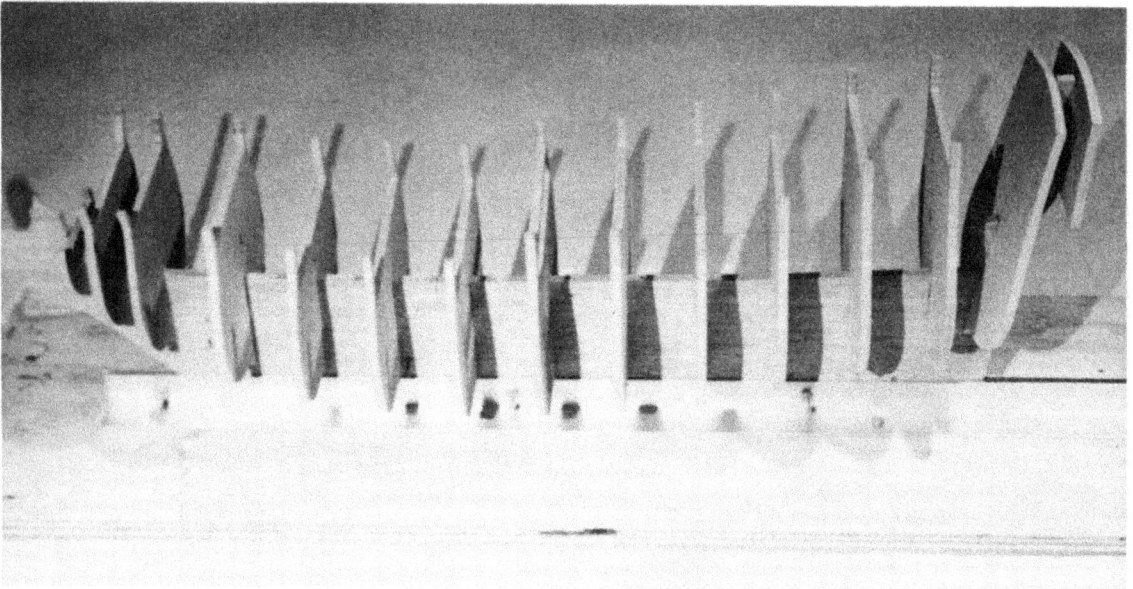

Fig. 1-6. My version of Dick Roos' aluminum keel holder, which is adjustable.

Fig. 1-7. The plank-bending jig in operation. The planks are left in the jig overnight and then removed to use in planking the bow area.

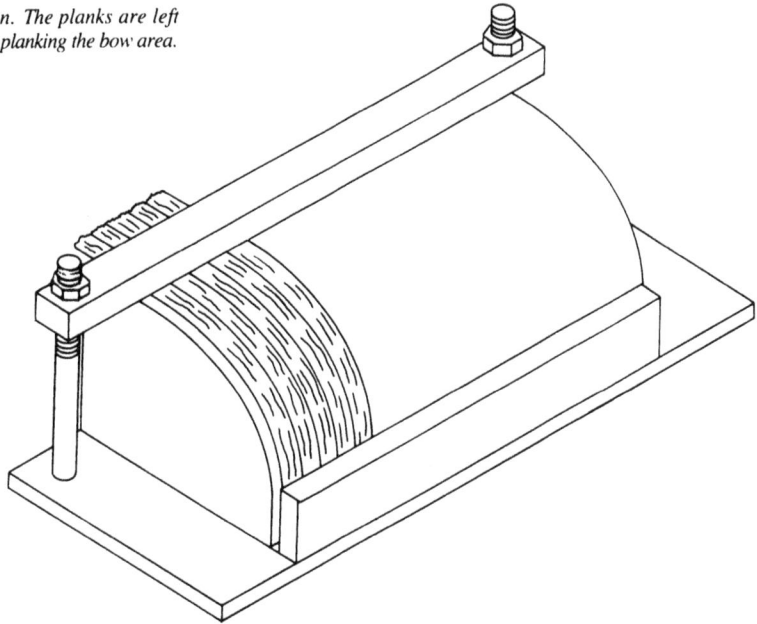

to the plans furnished with the kit. They can be traced off the body plan of the ship (FIG. 1-10) and used to hold up to the solid hull to verify the correct shape at that point.

Treat plank-on-bulkhead kits in the same way. The bulkheads themselves will be the templates, and they should be compared to the plans to make sure they are of the correct shape.

The power fretsaw is another tool that many of modelers only dream about because it is so expensive. The cheaper versions of this saw, such as the Dremel scroll saw, are not accurate enough for most ship modelers when trying to cut the hard woods used for the models.

Bob Saddoris, of the Ship Modelers Association, has modified the Dremel by installing a door spring on the top lever of the saw, which increases the tension on the blade. This tension makes the blade cut the wood more accurately and smoothly. The more costly types of fretsaw, like the unit built by Hegner, already have this and other features built in. This particular tool for scratch builders and advanced kit builders is a great help to modelers. Frustration can only result if your tool cuts your wood crooked.

Another power saw used by Bob Saddoris is the band saw. Try to cut out an accurate shape of a solid-hull ship without one. Again, these power tools just

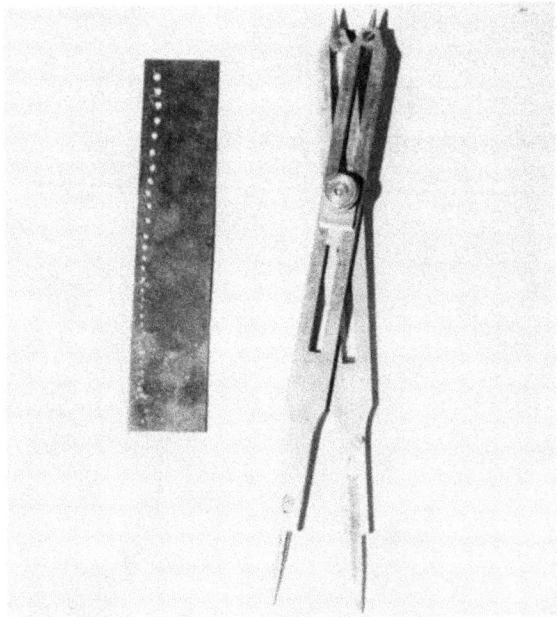

Fig. 1-8. My proportional dividers and one of the drawplates used to make dowels with.

make the job faster, and can give the modeler accurate results without the great deal of labor required if sawing by hand.

9

Fig. 1-9. Use templates such as these to make sure the solid-hull model you are building is of the proper shape at the indicated frame. You need one template for each frame of the model.

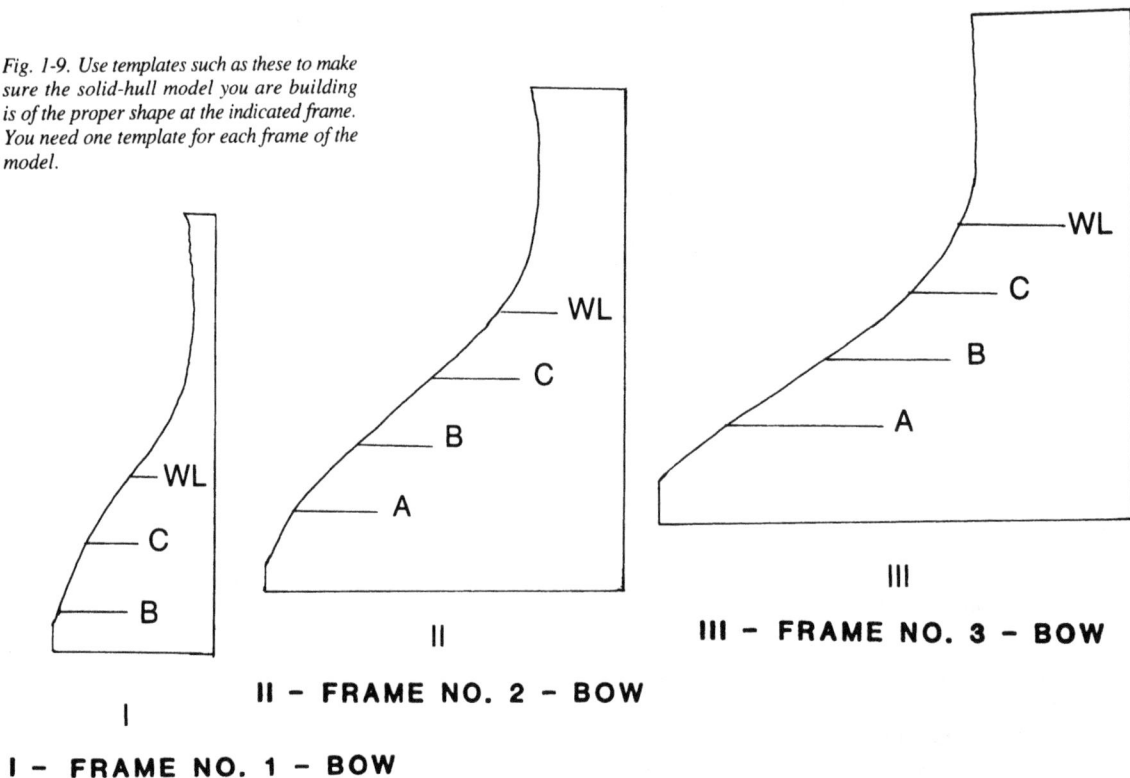

I

I - FRAME NO. 1 - BOW

II

II - FRAME NO. 2 - BOW

III

III - FRAME NO. 3 - BOW

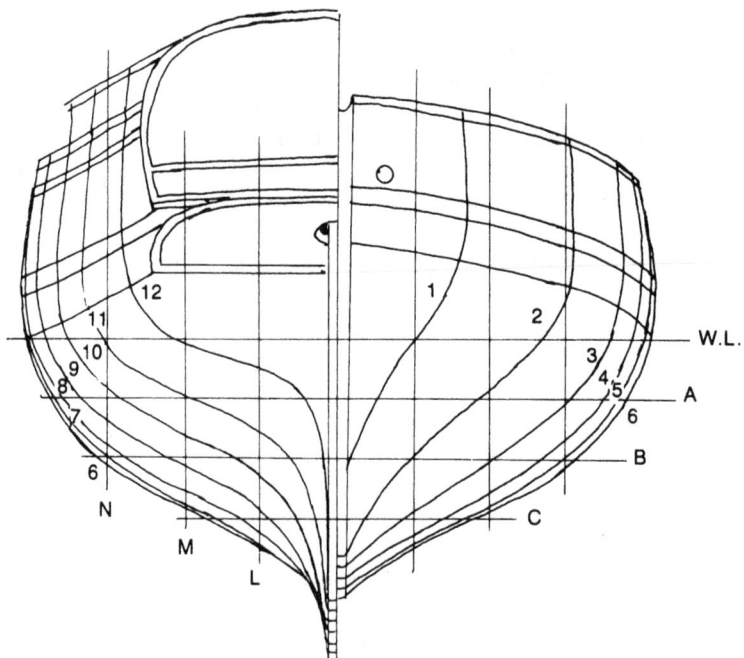

Fig. 1-10. A typical body plan of a ship model. This plan and the other drawings of the model are essential to making an accurate model of a ship.

There are those modelers who do everything by hand, scorning the power tool for a number of reasons. While I admire these individuals, I wonder what they could make if they took full use of modern technology. The joy in modeling is in the doing, however, and if you enjoy working with hand tools, then so be it.

One final tool I find indispensable is my magnifier. The one I am using attaches to my glasses and enables me to see what it is I am attempting to do. For the modeler who is blessed with excellent eyes and can see all the little details while he is working, they will not be of much help. For the rest of us, however, they are a real necessity.

2

Hull Structure

THE BASIC HULL STRUCTURE UPON WHICH THE planks will be placed is the topic of this chapter. The first thing to consider, for solid, plank-on-bulkhead and plank-on-frame methods of ship modeling, is the shape of the hull. The hull's shape is determined from the ship lines, which are obtained from the ship plans. Unfortunately, plank-on-bulkhead kits do not have a set of the ship lines shown on the plans. Their kits depend on the bulkheads supplied in the kit to give the modeler this information.

The solid-hull kits do give you this type of information. The ship lines are indicated in FIG. 2-1. This information is also of prime importance to the scratch builder. A full understanding of these lines and what they mean is a requirement of all serious model builders.

Item 1A of FIG. 2-1 shows the ship's sections or *body plan*. These are the lines used to make your templates referred to in Chapter 1. The elevation, or *sheer plan,* is shown as Item 1B of FIG. 2-1, and Item 1C shows the *half-breadth plan,* or waterlines. In 1A all three types of lines are indicated. *A* indicates the sections, *B* the sheer plan, and *C* the waterlines. The same letters in diagram 1B and 1C show the same lines.

It is just like taking a hull and cutting it up in different directions to see what it looks like. Each intersection of the lines gives you a specific point on the hull, which is located in three-dimensional space. And you thought ship modeling was simple. Now you begin to realize that ships are one of man's most complex constructional accomplishments.

Each line should be given an individual number. If you study the plans, you will see that this is the case. In the body plan drawing of Item 1A, the left side represents the forward part of the ship and the right side represents the aft part of the ship.

PREPARATION OF A SOLID HULL

Once you understand the lines, you can sand the solid hull supplied in the kit, and carve it to its final shape. To be perfectly accurate, you must also remove the amount of wood on the solid hull that will correspond to the thickness of the planking material you will plank the hull with.

Do not forget to use your templates made from the plans, as indicated in Chapter 1, to help shape your hull accurately. Again, these templates are made from the body plan information contained in 1A. FIGURE 1-10 shows a template example.

Most solid-hull kits do not come with planking material, so you will need to make it or purchase it in a good hobby shop. You can make the model without planking the hull if you are going to paint the model. You will not have the planked-hull effect if you do

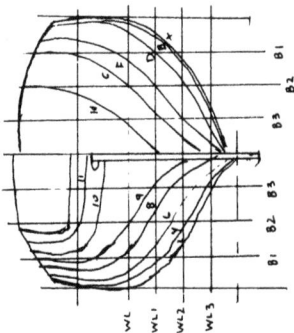

I A
BODY PLAN

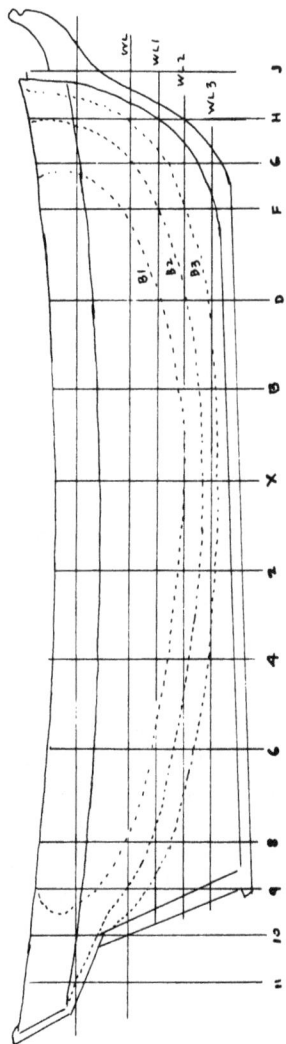

I B
SHEER PLAN

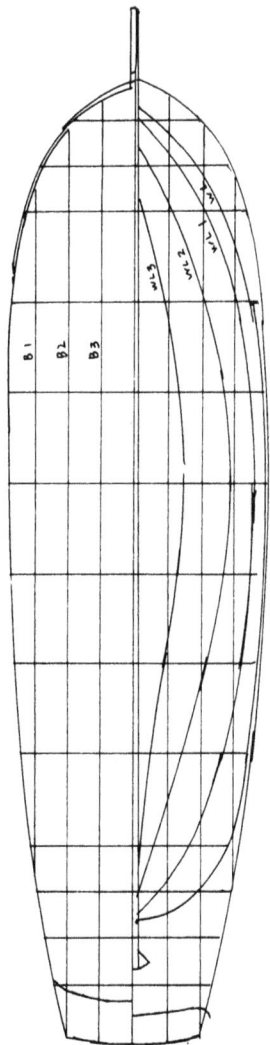

WATERLINES PLAN
I C

Fig. 2-1. Typical plan set for a ship. This is the minimum plan requirements needed to build an accurate ship model hull prior to planking it.

not plank, however. The solid-hull model does not look good if left in a natural state without painting or planking.

To remove the added thickness of wood, increase the size of the template to compensate for the size of your plank. Plane the surface of the hull level to where the keel will be installed. Remove the excess wood with wood rasps, power sanders, and chisels. If you remove too much wood, fill in with a good wood filler like Elmer's Professional Woodcarpenter's wood filler. The good wood fillers will sand just like real wood and not leave a hollow or bump. Hollow out the inside of the solid-hull kit as directed in the instructions.

Some of the Ship Modelers Association members have cut the bulkheads or walls all the way down to the deck and installed false frame timbers in their place, thus making the model a kind of half solid/half plank-on-frame model. Smooth the entire hull to a good finish and cut all gun ports, scuppers, etc. into the hull before you begin planking.

If you are building a solid-hull model, install the keel, stem, and sternpiece after you smooth out the hull and make it ready for planking. Also, it is easier to knock out the stern end of the model and replace it with a separate piece of wood, or plank it, as desired. The solid hull is now ready for planking. Use the templates to give it a final check.

PREPARATION OF A PLANK-ON-BULKHEAD HULL

The preparation of the plank-on-bulkhead type of ship model, be it kit or scratch, follows a different path. First prepare the keel, stem, and sternpiece between glass, as mentioned in Chapter 1. Again, be sure that there is no warping of your keel or any of the pieces that make it up. You must have a perfectly straight and true keel. Next, set the model up on your baseboard, as discussed in Chapter 1.

The next step is to install the bulkheads onto the keel structure. Be sure you check the bulkhead shape with the plans to make sure they match.

Put together the entire skeleton structure for your ship without glue to ensure that all parts fit properly. In addition to the keel and bulkheads, you should use some form of bracing to ensure the structure is locked together and will not move. Once you have made sure that all parts of the structure fit together properly, remove them and reinstall them using the glue. You can use dowels at this point if you are still concerned about the strength of your structure.

Install any filler pieces, particularly at the bow and stern, at this time. You should contour the filler pieces and the bulkheads to fit the shape of the hull and true it up as shown in FIG. 2-2. If you accidentally remove too much wood from one bulkhead or there is not enough bulkhead there despite your checking with the plans, then you must add wood, as indicated in FIG. 2-3.

You can check the correctness of this part of the construction program by laying a plank against the bulkheads running fore and aft. Make sure it makes contact with all the bulkheads without being rough or bumpy. The plank should be a smooth run from the stem to the sternpiece. The skeleton also should be perfectly symmetrical. The right side must be a mirror image of the left side.

In many kits, you will also fit your false deck at this time. Make sure your camber is right on the top of your bulkheads and on any deck beams you are to put in place. Some kits call for you to plank the deck at this time. The planking of the decks will be covered in Chapter 4. If all has been completed up to this point, you should have a skeleton that looks similar to FIG. 2-4. This kind of construction is also used by the scratch builder who is going to plank the entire hull and does not want to make the frames, as described later in this chapter.

One jig you can use while installing your bulkheads to make sure they are perfectly straight and square to your keel is the framing clamp. Dick Roos has made a framing clamp called the "Riteangle Ribb Rigger," which consists of a 7-ply birch veneer with a slot cut in it to fit over the keel of your ship kit (FIG. 2-5). The side of the framing clamp rests against the bulkhead to ensure perfect right-angle alignment with your keel. The block should have two coats of a wood sealer plus a hard wax finish to keep it from sticking to the keel or bulkhead. A hole is drilled in one side to accommodate a finger/winged bolt to secure the clamp to the keel. Two of these blocks can be used on each side of the bulkhead for perfect alignment.

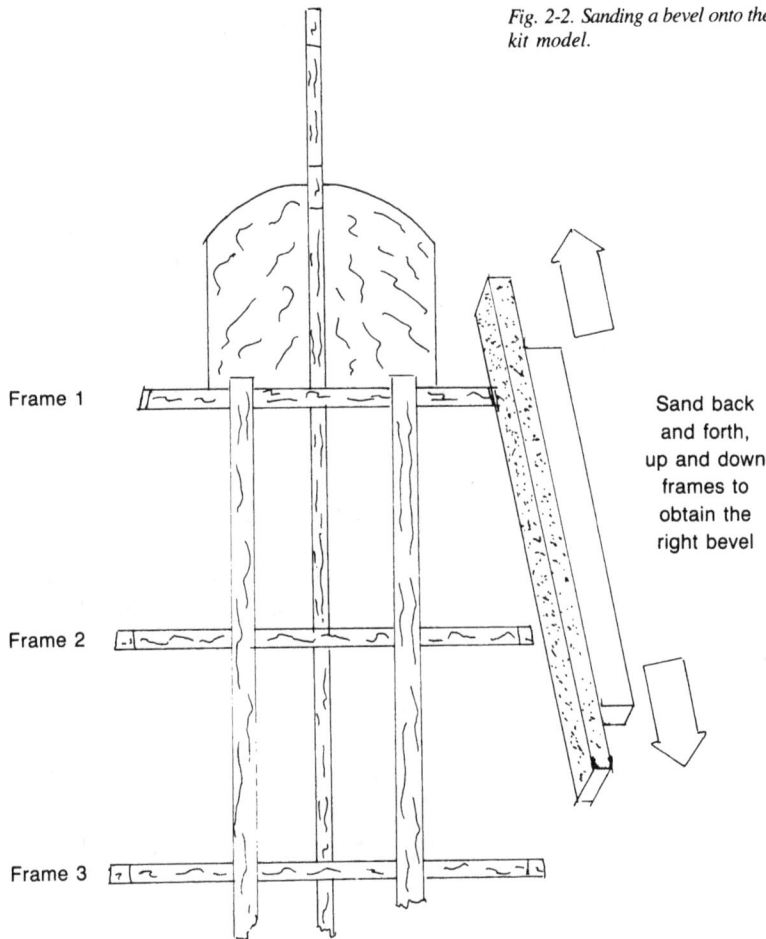

Frame 1

Sand back
and forth,
up and down
frames to
obtain the
right bevel

Frame 2

Frame 3

The little bits of information, such as the ''Riteangle Ribb Rigger,'' which I have obtained from the members of the Ship Modelers Association of Fullerton over the years has proved invaluable to me. I would strongly recommend that you join a local ship model club or form one of your own if none exists. This can be of great help to the scratch builder, as well as the novice ship modeler and the kit builder.

SCRATCH BUILDING

The scratch builder has a choice to make at the beginning of his construction. Is the model going to be solid and planked; plank-on-bulkhead, which requires a fully planked hull; or plank-on-frame, which will leave some of the planking off of the model to show the frames? The scratch builder who builds a model plank-on-frame and then planks the entire hull is basically wasting his time, since no one will see his frames.

There are several different methods and styles of making the plank-on-frame model. These variations start with the frame itself. Is the model going to be Admiralty fashion, or will it be built like the real thing? If Admiralty fashion, there are a number of different construction methods on building the frames of the ship model. I will outline the methods used by myself and other members of the Ship Modelers Association in planking wooden ship models.

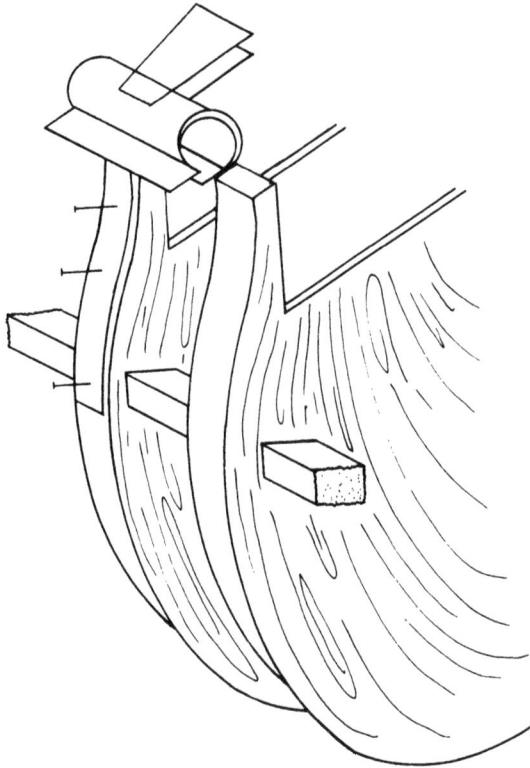

Fig. 2-3. A piece of wood is being added to the bulkhead to enable a clean run of the plank. If the piece of wood were not added, there would be a hollow space at this location. Check all bulkheads as indicated in the text to ensure a smooth run of your ship's hull planking.

SHIP MODEL KITS

One thing I should mention before I get any further with the construction methods is the degree of difficulty of some types of ship models over others in reference to the shape of the hull. The clipper-type ship with the pointed bow is not as difficult to plank as is the round, bluff-bowed ships like a large ship of the line. A modeler who is just getting started should consider building a clipper-type schooner like the *Harvey* by Artesania Latina or the *Shenandoah* by Corel. Both of these kits are plank-on-bulkhead with relatively easy lines to plank.

That is not to say that a beginner cannot plank a more difficult hull shape. I have seen it done. The primary thing is that you must like the model you are about to build. If you have no real interest in the model, you will probably not finish it. I think it also depends on your experience with other hobbies and how knowledgeable you are of woodworking.

There are over 84 kits of plank-on-bulkhead models available today, not to mention the over 80 solid-hull kits also sold. So, there is a large variety of ship model kits that can be purchased plus hundreds of plans available for the scratch builder. Go easy at first.

CONSTRUCTION OF FRAMES

The construction of frames for the ship model

Fig. 2-4. A skeletal frame structure of a typical plank-on-bulkhead model, the H.M.S. Unicorn by Corel. Notice the walnut addition to the keel and stem area, which replace the pressed wood furnished in the kit.

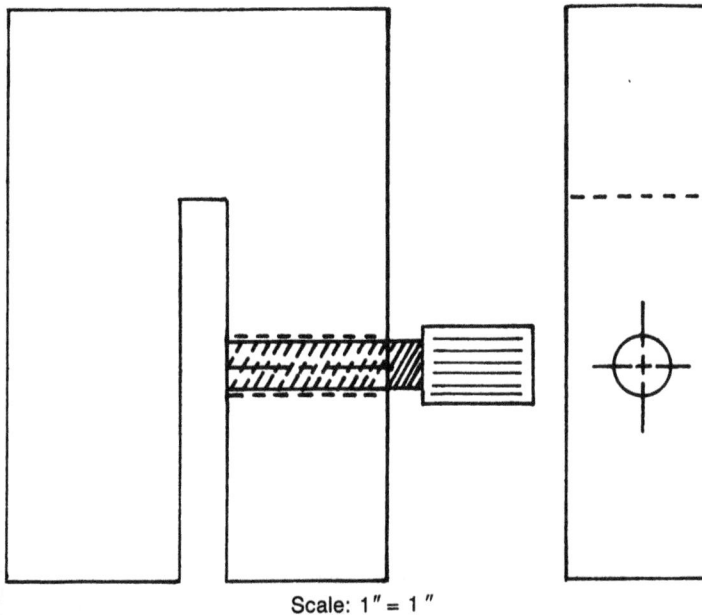

Scale: 1″ = 1″

Fig. 2-5. A scale drawing of Dick Roos' Riteangle Ribb Rigger. The slot goes into the ply keel with the flat side up against the bulkhead being installed. You can use two of these on both sides of the bulkhead to ensure it is straight and true to the keel. Give the block several coats of Deft to seal it and keep any excess glue from making it "stick" to the bulkhead or keel. You can size the finger/winged bolt shown to your choosing.

starts with the plans, but even prior to that with the construction of the keel for the frames. Again, the baseboard must be mentioned first.

Baseboard

Additional work is required on the baseboard to make life easier for construction of the frames. The first thing is to draw a centerline on the baseboard once you have sanded it smooth if this has not been done already. Then draw a second line in the middle of the board and perpendicular to the first line. This second line will indicate the center of your ship and will also identify the location of your center bulkhead or frame. Kit builders may do this also to ensure the accurate hull, although it is not as essential since the keels and ribs are basically already drawn out. This will be of great help if the kit builder is going to add additional frames.

An assumption is made that the scratch builder has already drawn out his plans and has all his frames numbered. This book is not intended to detail the fine points of draftsmanship. I will try to give a very brief idea of what is done to obtain the frame shapes from

the plans as I reach that stage. Here, the only thing that is required is to indicate your frames by number on the sheer plan (FIG. 2-1, Item 1B). The number of frames you will have for your ship again depends on what type of ship you are building—plank-on-bulkhead or plank-on-frame.

Plank-on-bulkhead does not require as many frames as plank-on-frame. As a general rule, there is one frame and then one space the equal size of the frame, then again one frame. This should be on your plans. Transfer the frame centerlines to your baseboard. It will help if you use a compass to draw these lines to make sure they are perfectly perpendicular to your keel centerline and absolutely true to each other. Also, inscribe them a little into the surface of the wood so you do not lose them in construction work at a later stage.

If you have chosen the solid-hull model or the plank-on-bulkhead type to scratch-build, then these are basically the same as the kit models, with the obvious exception that you will need to obtain the plans, make everything from scratch, and supply all you own materials.

Your main advantage in doing this is that you can select your own materials to work with. The disadvantage is that you do not have any instructions to assist you, and much of the rough work will have to be done by you, such as the basic shaping of the hull from stock wood using the *bread-and-butter* method, which is gluing the solid hull together with boards following the waterlines, or the plank-on-frame method.

Since this is to be a fully framed model, Dick Roos' aluminum keel holder might not work. You might need to build a holder similar to the one indicated in FIG. 2-6. Having already drawn your frame locations on the baseboard, cut some stock wood that is available, say ¼ × ¼ inch or whatever, and place along the keel location. Since you have already drawn your centerline, it will help to draw two parallel lines on either side of it, to which you will glue the pieces of wood that will make up your keel holder. The size of the keel will determine the spacing of the wood pieces, of course. Use a piece of the keel material to make sure it fits snugly before gluing. You might spend quite a bit of time on this baseboard, but you will find that it saves a lot of time and trouble later on.

Keel

Now you can start with the keel made of a piece of hardwood, which is longer than required since it should extend further out in both the bow and stern. Make sure that the keel is straight, is free from twists and bends, and is the right size.

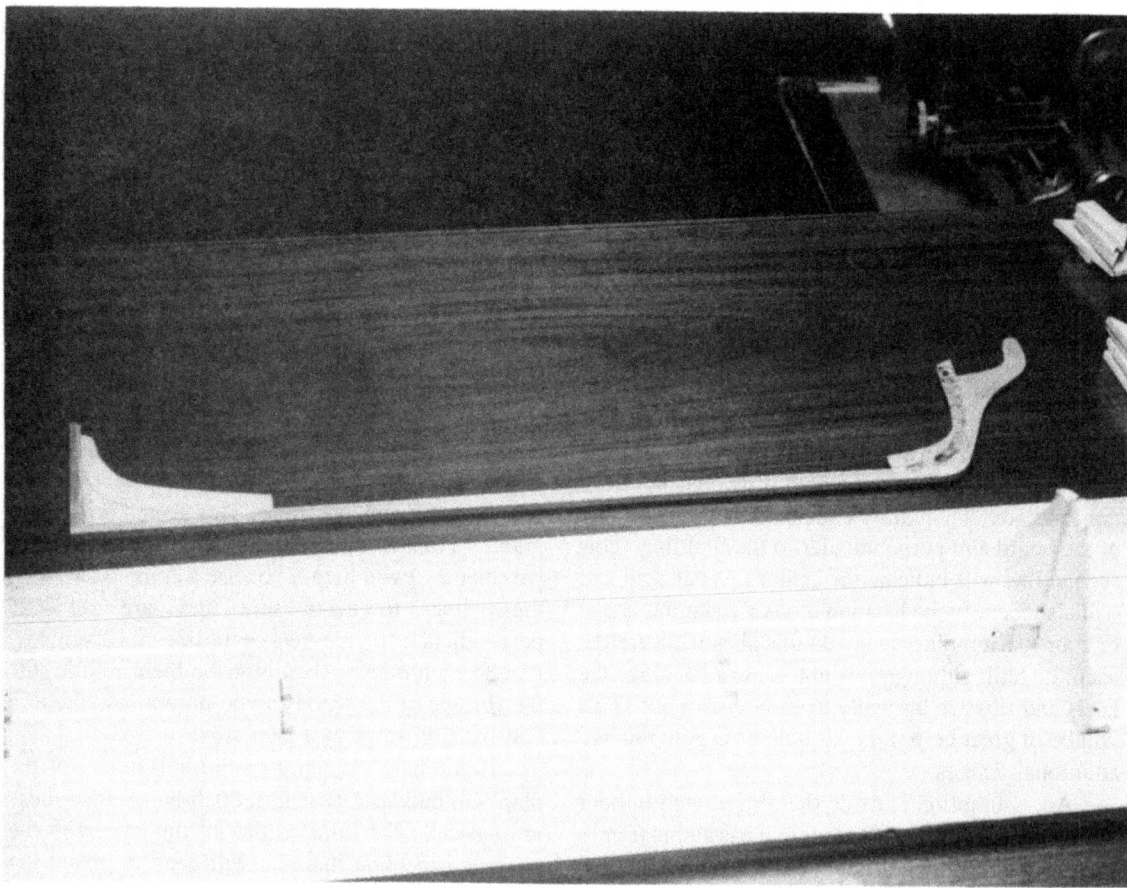

Fig. 2-6. Stem, keel, and sternpost structure with the building board marked out and braces in place. This is the beginning of the ship Conqueror, *scratch-built by Mr. Ed Marple.* (Photo courtesy of Ed Marple.)

Stem and Sternpost

You must now make the stem and sternpost skeleton parts. In kits they are made of plywood so the strength of the piece has been taken care of. In scratch-building you will not use plywood, so you must take care when building the stem and sternpost to ensure that they will be strong enough.

These two pieces of the skeleton of the ship must be made using separate pieces of wood to make sure the grain of the wood runs along the direction of the wood and not perpendicular to it. A curved stem, in particular, might be made up of four or five pieces of wood joined together with glue and wooden dowels. FIGURE 2-7 indicates the joined stem.

The wooden dowels have been mentioned before. Make them by drawing bamboo through a drawplate. The reason wooden dowels are used, in addition to the fact that this is what was used on the real ship, is because you might have to drill a hole through that particular location at a later stage in construction and if a nail is used it might prove to be difficult, if not impossible, to cut through the nail. Bamboo dowels are just as strong as nails when installed into the wood.

FIGURE 2-7 shows the stem construction. Trace the outline of the stem on tracing paper, with the joints drawn in. Place the drawing on a flat piece of plywood. Cover the drawing with a piece of wax paper, tacking the wax paper and the drawing down on the flat piece of wood. Next, cut your wood to the shape of the stem and each joint, making sure that the grain of the wood runs correctly (FIG. 2-7). Dry-fit all the pieces of wood that make up your stem.

When all the pieces fit properly, you are ready to glue the joints. Do not worry about the external shape of the stem at this point, just the joints and the run of the grain. Glue one joint at a time, and put the heavy glass over it to make sure it is flat, then when the glue has dried, dowel the joint together before you glue the next joint.

When all joints are doweled and glued, remove the wood from the wax paper and lift the drawing underneath from the board it was on. Cut out and attach the paper to the wood to use as a guide in cutting the external shape of the stem. Make the sternpost piece in the same way.

Scarf

Once made, take the keel, stem and sternpost, and lay them out on your drawing to show exactly where they are to join and where the scarfs are. Cut

Fig. 2-7. A close-up picture of the stem area of the ship model H.M.S. Unicorn *showing the removal of the kit-furnished plywood and replacement with the walnut.*

out these scarfs and glue the stem and sternpost together and then put them in between the two pieces of glass to let them dry overnight. Then dowel the joints firmly to the keel. The type of scarf to be used will depend on the ship you are building. Make sure that the keel still extends both forward and astern of your skeleton assembly.

Bow and Stern Holders

At this stage, a further addition is made to your baseboard, which is the bow and stern holders (FIG. 2-8). These are made out of hardwood. Be sure they are perpendicular to the centerline of the baseboard and that the slot cut in the holder is a snug fit for your stem and sternpost. Check with your plans to make sure just where to install these pieces on your baseboard.

Other Methods

There are other ways to make up your basic keel structure. I believe that there may be as many ways as there are modelers. A combination of plywood and a hardwood can be used to make a keel assembly that will have the advantages of the plywood strength, but will not show the plywood.

First, cut out the plywood keel to shape using your plan as a guide. Then select a hardwood that will represent the keel, stem, and sternpost. Lay the hardwood part that will form the keel even along the bottom of the plywood keel structure earlier cut out.

Now cut out both the hardwood part and the plywood keel together using a scarf cut. Glue the hardwood part onto the plywood part. Install the stern piece and the bow piece made from hardwood while removing the plywood parts. You are left with a plywood skeleton with the outside area made up of hardwood, such as boxwood or pear wood. Thus, the part of your model that will show is in the same wood as your planks, while the inside part of the structure is plywood. This type of construction is for ships that will be fully planked, of course.

This type of skeleton structure can also be used on kit type models to get rid of the plywood look of the keel, stem, and sternpost. All kits come with plywood keel structures. This type of construction is shown in FIG. 2-4.

Other Steps Required

On all of these methods of making the keel, stem, and sternpost structure, you must taper the keel, stem, and sternpost if called for in your plans. I know that not all of the kit models I have built have mentioned this point, but the structure was tapered from the center to the stem and the sternpost. This taper, if done, must be accurate and will require a centerline down the structure to ensure that everything is symmetrical (FIG. 2-9).

Another item that is seldom, if ever, mentioned in kit instructions is the fact that you must sand smooth

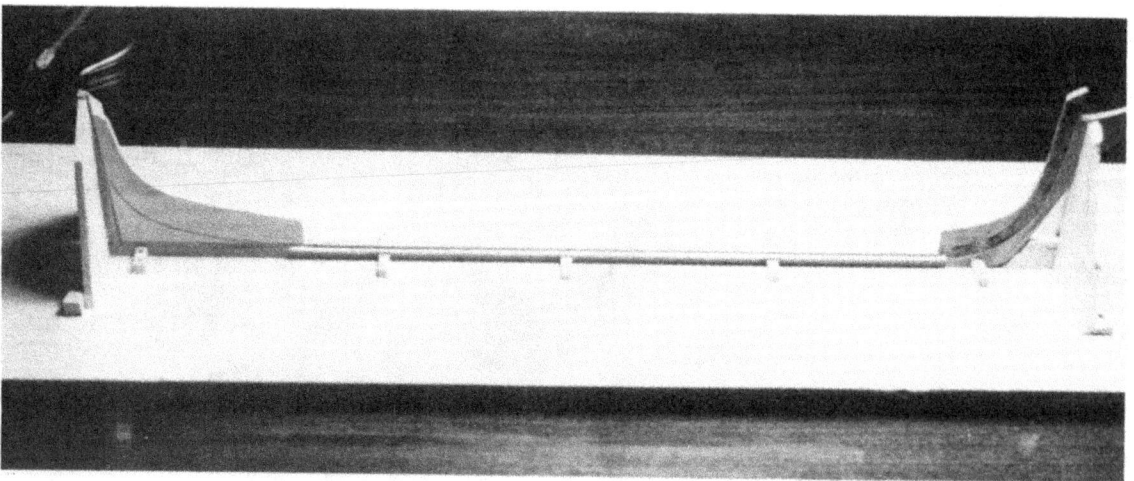

Fig. 2-8. The stem, keel, and sternpost of the ship Conqueror *in its building board.* (Photo courtesy of Mr. Ed Marple.)

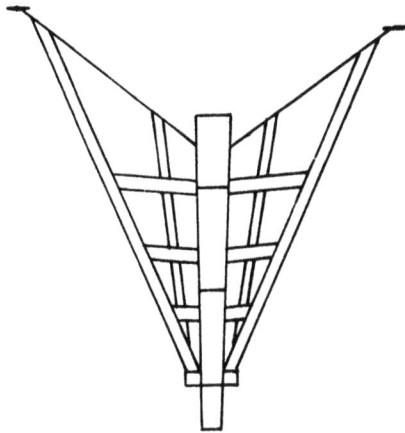

Fig. 2-9. Drawing of the head area of a ship, showing the taper of the stem from the part that connects to the hull to the tip of the head. This same taper is evident on the keel, the sternpost, and the rudder.

all parts of the ship structure as you proceed with your building. I guess this is considered self-evident by the kit makers. I find myself doing the same thing. Be sure to sand all finished parts before proceeding onto the next step of construction.

Another item that is not addressed in the instructions for ship kits is the inclusion of a rabbet cut into the keel structure. The *rabbet* is a groove cut into the wood where the planks will fit flush into the keel, stem, and sternpost structure already put together.

Obtain the rabbet lines from the plans and carefully draw them onto the keel structure prior to cutting. Great care must be taken here with the cutting of the rabbet. Cut the rabbet very carefully with an Uber or X-ACTO knife by hand; I know of no other way to do it. Also use files and rifflers to help cut the groove.

FIGURE 2-10 shows several areas where the rabbet is cut. Note the different shapes of the groove. The bow area, or curve, can be the most difficult area to cut, but use of a template made from a scrap piece of timber will aid you (FIG. 2-11). Wood is very forgiving and can be repaired if required, but care and patience will save you more work and frustration later on.

Also, take time out to see what you have done and to admire your efforts up to this point. If you see something wrong, do not ignore it, but do something to correct the problem. Racing on to the next step without looking back is not always the best way to

build a ship model, and will eventually lead you into trouble.

One thing I would like to stress very much before you get too far into the construction of the ship model is that you must pay very close attention to the scale of the model and follow that scale closely. When making measurements, be as accurate as you can be, and do not think that "a little bit off" is all right. A small difference of 1/16 inch in 1/4-inch scale (which is usually a larger scale than most kits) results in 1/4 foot in the real ship. This can mean a large difference if you are planking, since each error accumulates. It is hard to get port and starboard symmetry when there are errors in measurement. This will become even more apparent when you start to plank your ship.

Adding the Deadwood

You will have to install your deadwood if you are scratch-building a model using the plank-on-frame construction talked about earlier in this chapter. With the plywood-type construction, the deadwood area is already filled in with the plywood. This deadwood area is filler in the stem and sternpost part of the skeleton structure (FIG. 2-12). The area can be completed with scrap wood of the same thickness as the keel. Everything you do here should be doweled, as well as glued, just to make sure nothing comes apart at a later date. Your model should now look something like FIG. 2-8 on its building board.

Having finished the deadwood, you now place the completed skeleton keel assembly into your completed baseboard and admire your work up to this point. While doing so, check to make sure that you have done all required work, and start considering how you are going to tackle the next step.

If you are in doubt as to how to do something during the construction of the model, you might check on how they built the real ship. Sometimes following as closely as possible the real procedures that the shipwrights used is the best way to tackle a problem area. One of these problem areas is our next project, the stern construction.

CONSTRUCTION OF THE STERN

Even the kit modelers have a tough time with the stern area of the ship model. Again, there are almost

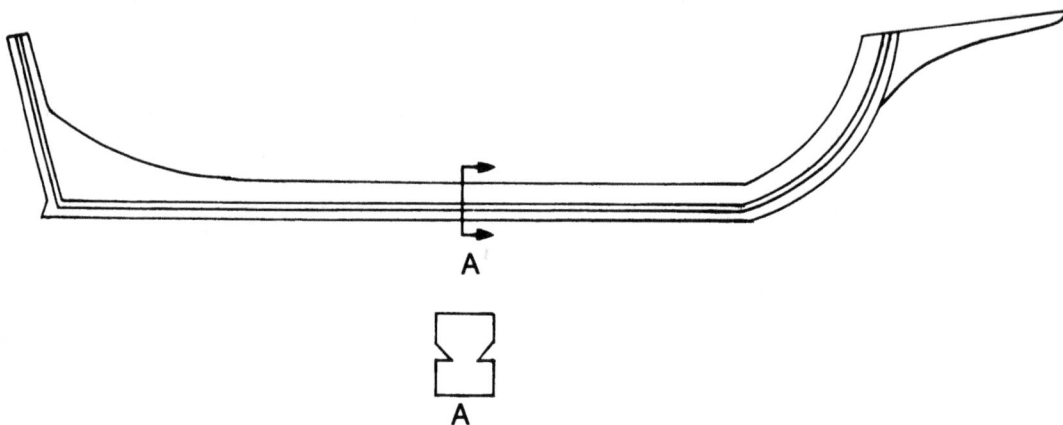

Fig. 2-10. A picture of the stem, keel, and sternpost structure showing the rabbet.

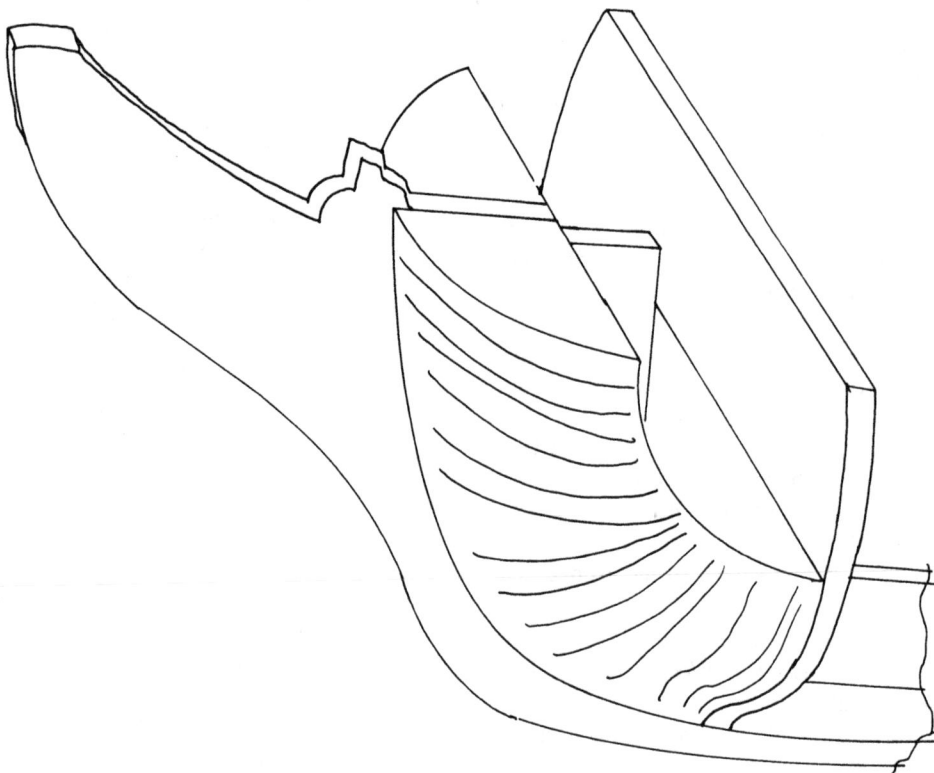

Fig. 2-11. One method of making sure your bow area will be planked the right way is to use blocks of wood as shown. Leaving this area with no support is inviting disaster when you start to plank.

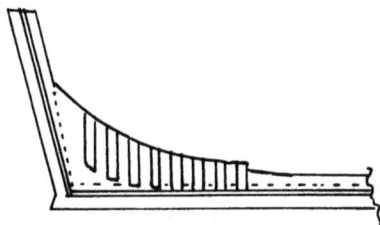

Fig. 2-12. The stern area showing the notches cut into the deadwood for the aft frames, along with the rabbet.

as many ways of doing this job as there are ship modelers, and there are many ways to do the kit model sterns. The kit builder can get away with more than the scratch builder since the kit builder will double-plank his model. If you are building a kit, double planking allows you to do more experimentation with the first layer.

Try to make your work as neat as possible even at this stage. Many kit-model instructions tell you to glue the pieces of wood and not pay attention to the gaps since these areas will be filled in at a later period with metal ornamentation. Do not assume that this is right because the instructions tell you so. Do not be afraid to vary from the kit and try your own idea if you think it is better than the kit instructions. You can and should add many details and improvements to your ship model kits to both improve their looks and accuracy.

If you are a scratch builder, you might decide to make the stern out of a block of wood that is attached to a false frame or bulkhead. To use this method, first make your block of wood out of different pieces of wood the same thickness as a frame. Alternate the wood grain in each piece since you will be cutting out the form of the stern timbers. Carve this block to the shape of the stern, then cut out from the block the pieces of wood not wanted, thus leaving the timbers of the stern standing proud. Use the false frame to hold the entire assembly together and to make sure everything is correctly symmetrical. Once this stern frame piece has been completed, you can install it on the ship's skeleton.

Since the whole stern structure was very fragile even on the real ship, it is one of the most interesting parts of the ship to build. Following the actual methods of ship construction, the first timber you need to construct is the wing transom, which along with the planks themselves, is the only item that held the stern together. Then fit the fashion pieces, and plank the stern below the wing transom. You can then wait until you have planked the hull before you fit the stern piece, which will be cut out of one piece of wood. Next, add the timbers above the deck. If your ship is a large one, you must install the lower deck transom and the transom pieces below it, followed by notching the side counter timbers. Then come the counter timbers, the upper deck transom, the quarter deck transom, the poop deck transom, and the stern timbers.

When you have reached the point that you can do a professional job on the stern of a large man-of-war, you have done what most modelers want to do. Careful study of the plans of the ship you are building, careful measurements taken of every area of the stern, and much thought as to how you are going to build up the stern are necessary to complete this challenging part of the ship model. Do not hesitate to stop and spend some time thinking about what you are going to do and how you will do it. There is no one way to do something. Each ship model you will build is different, providing new challenges to your skill.

The quarter gallery is often part of the stern decoration effort of the ship model and is mentioned here since it also can be a real problem to some modelers to try to construct. The best example I can give you is the model of the *Prince,* built by Mr. Ed Marple of the Ship Modelers Association (FIG. 2-13). It is built up from many pieces.

You can use many different methods of building the stern in addition to those indicated in this chapter. I know that the stern area can be one of the more difficult areas to figure out. The best advice that I can give is to either follow as closely as possible the real method of framing the stern or follow the method just outlined. You might need to spend a lot of time thinking and studying about the stern before you find your own solution. You might want to move on to the next chapter on planking your ship and plank the ship first before adding the stern, thus using the planks as a support for the stern.

FRAMES

The next step is to tackle the frames. Here we first come upon the requirement for scratch builders to have at least a good basic knowledge of drafting. You will have to first draw out your frames one by one.

The best way to do the actual frame drawing once you have obtained the points from the plans of the ship is to draw a *half frame*. By this I mean you should construct on paper a centerline and some station lines as reference. Then plot your points for the curve of the frame on one side only. Fold the paper in half along the centerline and make a tracing of the half already drawn on the other side. This method will ensure that both sides of the frame are identical.

This step is extremely important because you want the port side of your ship to be identical to the starboard side. Drawing the entire frame out, no matter how carefully, will probably lead to small errors since you will need to use a French curve.

It is also a good idea for the kit builder to check bulkheads for symmetry for the same reason. Most of the kit manufacturers do not make the components of the kit to exacting standards, and there are sometimes large areas of discrepancy with the kit-supplied bulkheads. Check both the bulkheads against the plans supplied and check the plans themselves by folding the bulkhead drawing in half and holding it up to a light to see if it is symmetrical or not. If it is not symmetrical, correct it now; it will give you problems later if you do not.

To assist in checking and drawing bulkheads and frames, you will need a boxlike affair with no bottom. On the top of this box, you should cut out a 1-×-1-foot square and insert a piece of glass or plastic. Inside the box, install a small light. You now have a small light table. Put the folded half frame drawing down on the glass and turn on the light so you can see the lines of the frame underneath and trace the other side of the frame. You can also use it to check the accuracy of the bulkhead drawings supplied in the kit.

After you have drawn out your frames or checked all of your bulkheads for accuracy, then you will make your new bulkheads if necessary and install the bulkheads, or you will make your frames and install them. FIGURE 2-14 shows construction methods for your frame. Each frame is made up of three parts: the floor, futtocks, and top timbers. Here again the

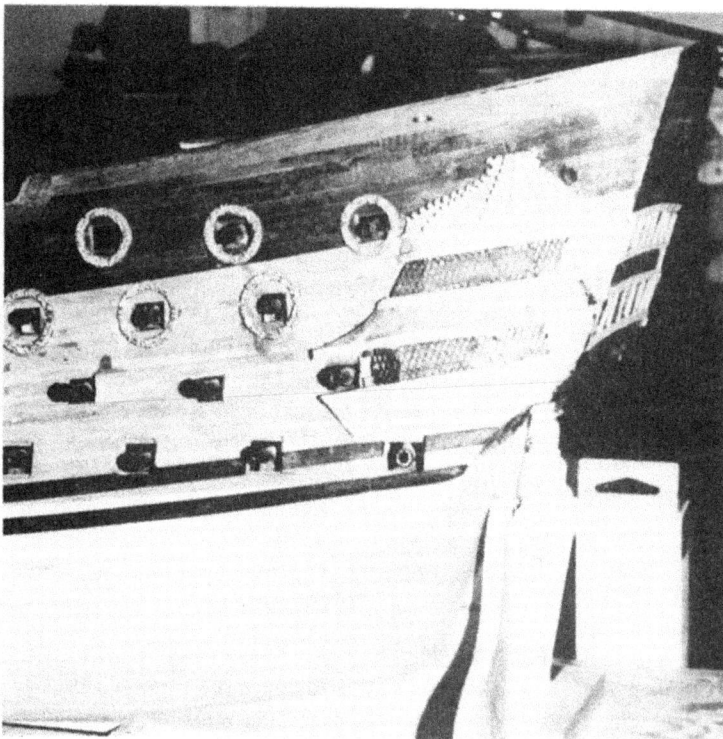

Fig. 2-13. The stern quarter of the ship H.M.S. Prince *under construction by Ed Marple. All of his models are scratch.* (Photo courtesy of Ed Marple.)

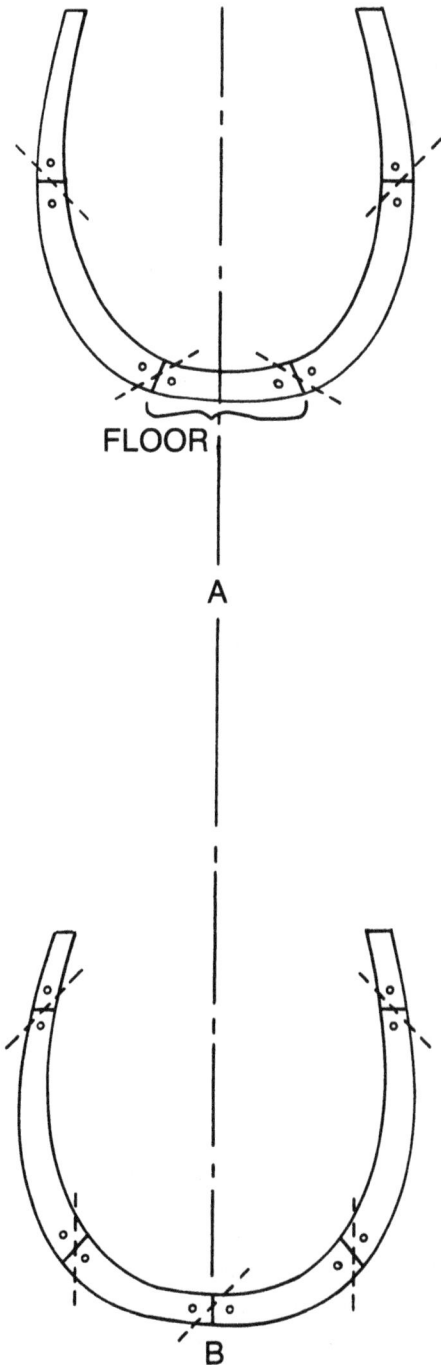

FLOOR

A

B

Fig. 2-14. A typical frame with part A being glued and doweled to part B. Notice that the joints are not in the same location on both parts of the frame.

grain of the wood is very important, and you should follow the practice used by the builders themselves to make sure your frames are strong enough to bear the stresses placed on them by the planks.

Tack the drawing to the board, then glue pieces of wood to the paper using rubber cement. Install the wood as shown in FIG. 2-14A, and insert dowels for strength. Then use wood glue to cement a second layer of wood to the first layer. Make sure the joints are at different locations from the first layer (FIG. 2-14B). Dowel all parts. You can install scarfs and the like if you so desire.

Remember, the frames will show up on the completed model. You can highlight the frames' layered construction process by using varying colors of wood when making the different sections of the frame. This is up to the individual modeler. Some modelers do not care for this treatment.

You next must decide whether or not to include the ship's bulwark stanchions as part of the frame. You can go either way, depending on your personal methods of construction. If you choose to make them part of the frame, however, you should include the bulwark stanchions in the drawing of the frame. You can also add them later on in the construction process if desired.

Another item that must be addressed is the inclusion of the bevel line on the frame drawing. Each frame must be beveled both on the outside and on the inside. Beveling is best done while you can hold the frame in your hand prior to installing it on the keel, especially for the inside part of the frame. To assist in making the proper bevel without taking off too much of the wood, draw a dark pencil line along the outer edge of the bevel. Do not exceed or eliminate this line. The bevel is very important, and time spent doing it as accurately as possible will save you a lot of time and trouble later. The planking of the hull and bulwarks will not come out right unless the bevel is done properly.

ACTUAL FRAME CONSTRUCTION

The actual frame construction, from the start to the end, will be demonstrated just to make sure you understand the concept. You started by drawing out

WATER LINES

BUTTOCK LINES

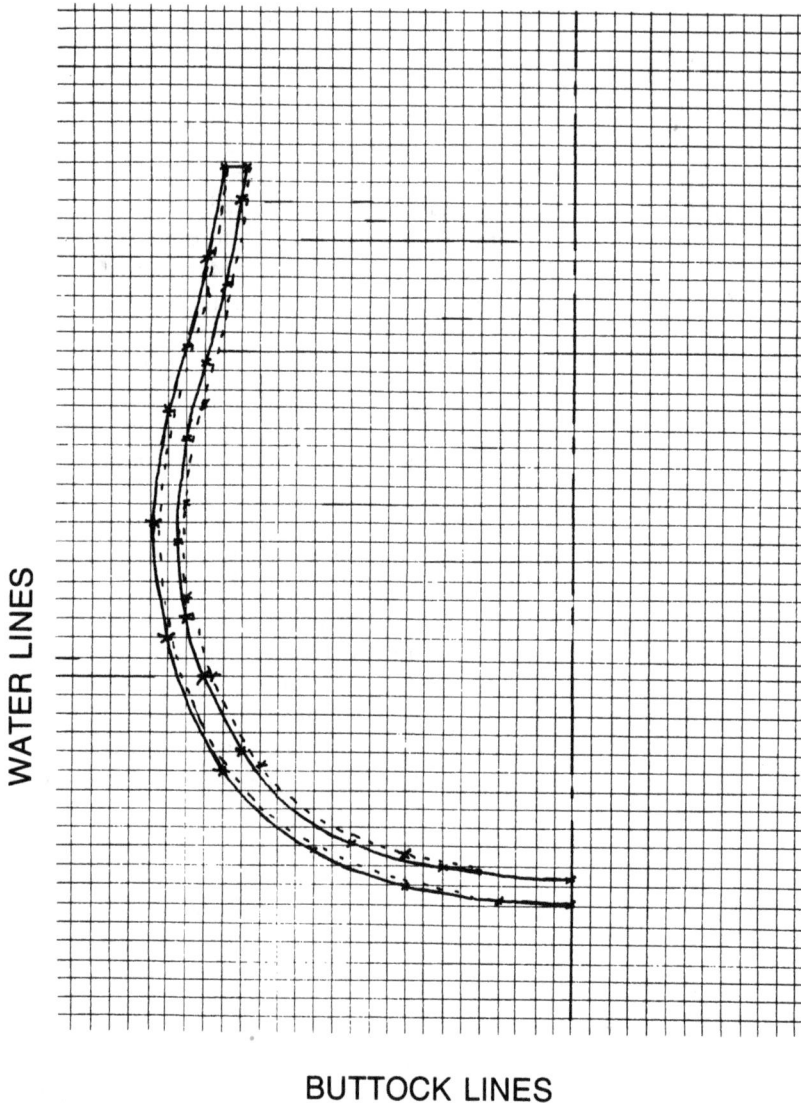

Fig. 2-15. A picture of a frame being taken off of the plans, as discussed in the text. The x marks are the points that have been taken from the junction of the waterlines and the buttock lines of the ship's plans, as shown in Fig. 2-1. Only half of a frame is needed.

your frame. This is an area that will give some people a lot of trouble, so I will try to explain in detail one way you can remove the points from the *ship lines drawings* and draw out your frame. The ship lines drawings are the three views of the ship talked about earlier in this chapter: the body plan or *sections plan*, the sheer plan or *profile plan*, and the half-breadth plan or *waterlines*.

The frame spacing has to be decided on and is usually what is called *Room and Space rule*, which

means that you have a frame, in my case made up of two thicknesses of wood, then a space of air the equal thickness of your frame, then another frame. To help you, the frame faces, or *planes*, are defined. Part of the frame that the plank will be attached or fastened to is called the *sided size* front and back. The part of the frame that does not have a plank attached to it is the *molded size*.

The lines drawings will not show all the ship's frames because this would result in a mass of lines, which would not make any kind of sense. Only a few lines are actually drawn on your typical plan.

The best plans are obtained from a museum or good book on ship modeling. Most kit plans in plank-on-bulkhead kits do not have proper lines drawings. Some of the better solid-hull kits do. The scratch builder might like to know that these plans can be purchased separately and used to make excellent models of the plank-on-frame type.

For the modeler who has a plank-on-bulkhead kit and wants to improve it by adding frames instead of using the kit-provided bulkheads, you can draw up your own set of lines drawings, first using the bulkheads provided in the kit as a guide. For the lucky kit builder who is furnished with these plans, some of the work has already been done for you. You can also try to obtain another set of plans of the model you are building from a museum, then reduce these plans to the scale of your kit—since most museum plans are available in ⅛-inch and ¼-inch scale only—and proceed to make the frames this way.

Having obtained the lines drawings, the other items you require are good drafting paper, a pair of compasses, a French curve or two, and a good straightedge. One other item is a pencil. You should use a good, hard-lead pencil, at least a No. 6 lead. You might have to go to some length to obtain this hard a pencil, but the fine lines it draws will serve you well in your construction. Even the thickness of the pencil line can result in errors of size, which will hurt you in your effort to construct an accurate ship model. Besides, the No. 6 lead is also very clean and does not make as much of a mess as the softer leads.

Transferring Points

The next step is to remove the points from the lines drawings to a clean piece of paper to establish your frame shape. First place the sheer plan—which indicates the side of the ship and shows the waterlines and the section lines as straight lines—and the waterline plan—which shows the section lines and buttocks as straight lines—one above the other. The section lines should match up and result in the same lines when a straightedge is laid down across both drawings.

You must use the Room and Space rule to establish the centers of your frames. If your frame is ¼ inch in thickness measured on the sided size, then your center is ½ inch, which is the distance from the center of one frame to the next frame. Now, measure off along the uppermost waterline of the sheer plan ½-inch points from the midship's station line. To be sure you are accurate, since these lines will represent one face of each of your frames, do the same thing along one of the section lines of your half-breadth plan. Then draw the lines through both plans with your straightedge.

Next form a grid pattern that is the same as the body plan of the ship. Use the waterlines and buttock lines as the straight lines and place the keel in the middle of the grid. To make things a little easier, you can line up this grid pattern with the waterlines of the sheer plan, but this step is not that important since you will be making a grid pattern for each frame. It would save you some work if you have access to an accurate photocopying machine. The unit must be absolutely accurate or errors will creep in, so be sure your grid is true.

You now have everything necessary to make the drawing of your frame. First, measure the distance with your compass from the centerline to the highest waterline of your half-breadth plan for the frame you wish to draw. Just to make sure you do not make any mistakes, identify all your frames with numbers or letters on the drawings. It is easy enough to get lost with all those lines, so label each line. Use your compass to transfer this distance to the grid pattern, putting the needle of your compass on the centerline of the keel and your compass mark on the waterline on both sides of the centerline. Do this same procedure for each waterline until you have made a mark for each waterline.

Next, proceed to the sheer plan. From the baseline or rabbet line, measure up to the point of the first buttock line. Locate this distance on your grid pattern on both sides of the centerline. Again, do each buttock line until you have done them all.

The last step is for you to measure from the rabbet line up to the rail line. Mark this with a special mark on both sides of your centerline since this line will be transferred to your frame and will become a strong reference point. Do the same thing with your deck line. It would not hurt to add more points, such as

Cant-frame spacing
same as square frame: x = x

First seven frames
are cant-frames

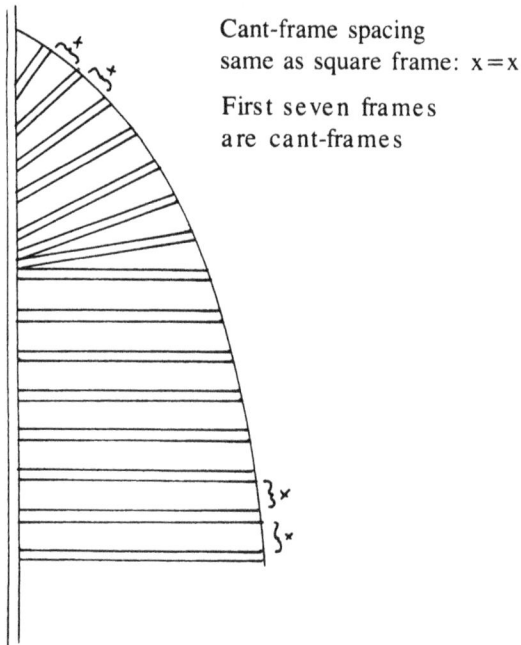

Fig. 2-16. The cant frames laid out showing the proper spacing required, as well as the sharp bevel of the ends of the cant frames making contact with the keel, deadwood, and stem area. Notches must be cut into the deadwood to accept these frames.

the wale line, especially if the ship being built is a large one.

Finishing the Drawing

You now can connect all these points using a French curve to get a picture of your frame. A lot of this work is not necessary, however. Remember, I used half-frame drawings, folded the drawing in half, and traced the other half.

The copying of the other half eliminates one-half of the drawing work. It might not seem like much, but remember also that this is only one line of your frame. You still have to draw the other half of the molded size picture of your frame, along with the inside and outside bevel. You are also not prone to make a small error while moving the compass from one side of your grid drawing to the other side. Also, I do not know how you can be sure that the French curve line you draw on one side is identical to the line you draw on the other side, since even a slight alteration of the position of the French curve will re-

sult in different line curves. FIGURE 2-1 shows the ship's lines, while FIG. 2-15 shows a typical grid pattern with a curve drawn in. FIGURE 2-16 shows the sequence for a cant frame, which is one of the harder frames to construct properly because of the sharp curves involved.

Using the rabbet line of the keel as the baseline makes the assumption that the plans are drawn to the inside of the planking of the model. You must be careful drawing in the cant frames at the bow and stern. They are not straight as are the other frames and must be treated in a slightly different manner. The stern might not have any cant frames, but the bow always will have them. Draw them in on the half-breadth plan at an angle so that the outer face of the frame is flush with the run of the planking on the model (FIG. 2-17). These frames are half frames and will be fixed to the deadwood of the keel. You can draw them out the same way as the regular frames once you have drawn them on the plans.

Using this Method for Plank-on-Bulkhead

This same procedure can be followed if you are a plank-on-bulkhead builder, with the advantage that you do not have to worry about the inside shape of the frame, only the outside form. Also, I have used this same method on kit models of plan-on-bulkhead type by drawing my own set of ship lines drawings, using the bulkheads supplied in the kit and the keel structure as references. In this way, you can add more bulkheads to the kit model, especially since some of the kits do not have enough of the bulkheads supplied with them.

If there are not enough bulkhead pieces in the kit, then it is very hard to plank without getting a lot of hollows and bumps in your planking. Even if you are using a double-plank method, it is still a lot of work to try to make the first layer of planking smooth and fair in order to apply the second layer of planking. I think it is easier to add a few more bulkheads at the beginning and avoid this problem.

The bow area is a problem area with a lot of modelers. Installing additional cant bulkheads would tend to make the job a lot easier. I have found that balsa wood fillers in the bow and stern are not much help and might even be a problem. If your ship kit is supplied with balsa wood, discard it. Substitute another softwood and you will have a lot less trouble when you begin to plank.

Drawing the Rest of the Frame

Draw out the rest of the frame using the same methods outlined previously. You will need to scribe more lines to represent the faces of your frames. Measure forward the thickness of your frames that are forward of the midship's line and aft the thickness of your frames that are aft of the midship's line. This enables you to remove the bevel from your frames, not have to add it on as you would one the aft portion of the model if the lines were taken off forward for the thickness of your frames aft. This completes your drawing efforts, and you can now make all the frames for your ship model.

There is one more item you can add to your keel structure. (I obtained this idea from Henry Bridenbecker.) It is a piece of wood along the keel with notches cut in it for the frames. These notches have to be carefully taken off the ship's plans where the frames locate into the ribs. It would help to label each frame notch along with each frame to make sure you have not missed a frame or put one out of place.

STRUCTURAL RIGIDITY

Another problem area with kit models is the rigidity of the rib or bulkhead structure once the bulkheads have been put in place. Some of the kits take this problem in hand and build in structural bracing of some kind, such as a dowel on both sides of the keel inserted through holes already installed in the bulkheads.

Many kits, however, have no bracing other than the false deck that is installed at this time. This false deck is usually not enough to rigidly brace the bulkheads together. If you have one of these types of kits, I suggest that you add some form of bracing to the keel and bulkhead structure.

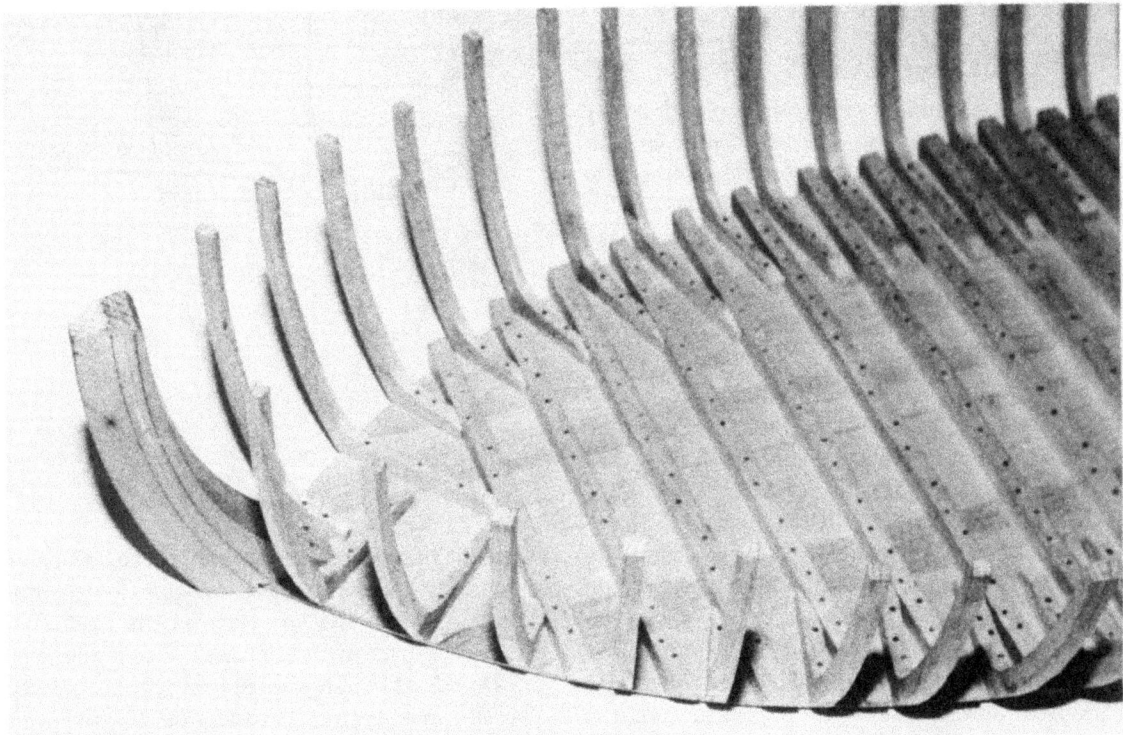

Fig. 2-17. An example of the need to make sure the frames are flush with the run of the planking. This photograph is of Dave Yotter's model of the Philadelphia, a gondola gun boat used in the American Revolutionary War.

This is one reason you should always fit everything together before gluing. If your structure is not rigid, you can put all the bulkheads together in clamps, being sure to correctly align the frames. Place the clamped together frames into a drill press and drill two holes through them on either side to enable you to insert a dowel down both sides. You must draw centerlines on all of the bulkheads to make sure they are all lined up properly. When you release the bulkheads from the clamp and reinstall them in their proper place on the keel, you can run two dowels through the drilled holes to add strength and to make sure the frames do not move while you are planking.

Another way of doing the same thing is to cut square notches on either side of the bulkhead and install square braces the entire length of the keel.

With either method, carefully study your plans to make sure that these braces are not installed in a location on your hull that will cause you trouble later, such as where your gunports or a deck will be located. You now have a rigid and strong structure to which you can plank your model.

SUPPORTING FRAMES

The scratch builder must come up with a way of supporting his frames. Henry Bridenbecker uses a modified form of the jig procedure discussed in Harold A. Underhill's book, *Plank-on-Frame Models and Scale Masting and Rigging, Vol. I.* You can make more than one of the frame jig described here if the ship you are constructing is a large one.

This jig is one of the most important jigs in the entire construction process for this method of frame construction. It is obtained from the deck-level waterline (half-breadth) plan. It is the waterline nearest the deck level and the wale. FIGURE 2-18 indicates this frame jig with the notches cut in for each frame, the keel, and the sternpost.

Be sure to make this jig absolutely accurate. A centerline is of course required, followed by notching out the stem and sternpost locations and fitting the board to make sure it goes at its proper location. At this point, in order to avoid problems of the jig rocking or moving sideways and to make sure it is perfectly level, add two or three absolutely true boards to the jig at the bottom perpendicular to the

Typical frame jig

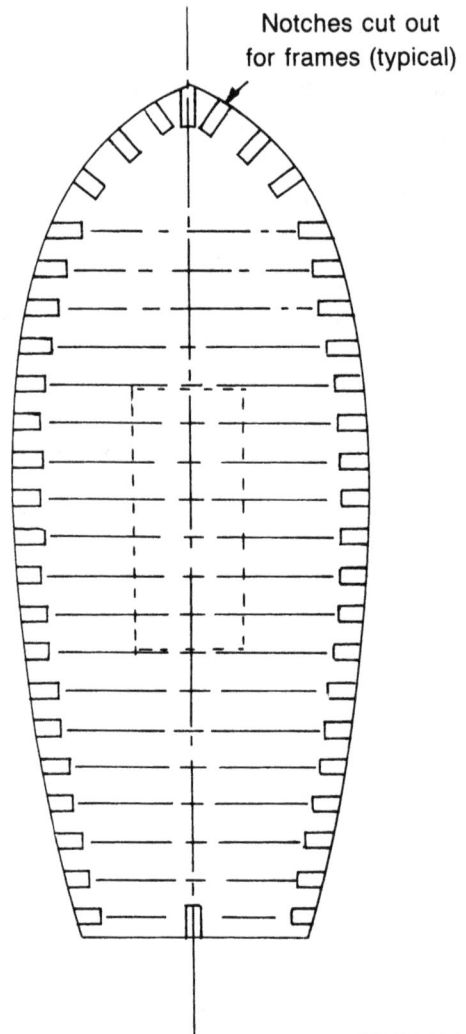

Notches cut out
for frames (typical)

Fig. 2-18. A drawing of a typical frame jig. Notice the notches cut for the cant frames at the bow. This jig is best made from a good-quality five-ply birch veneer or an equivalent material.

centerline of the jig and extending all the way down to your baseboard. To make sure that the length is correct, measure the "height" boards from your plans. Cut a notch in each of these boards for the keel.

Do not add these parallel boards to the jig yet. You still must cut out the waterline form and the notches of the frames. Draw all of these items on the jig first, then cut the outline of the hull at the waterline chosen, thus giving you the jig with a hull shape at the waterline and two notches cut in it at the bow and stern. Your frame locations are indicated, so cut these out, too.

When the notches are cut in the jig, remember to consider the thickness of your outer planking and the thickness or molded size of your frames at this waterline. Then make sure each notch fits the stem and sternpost locations, and take measurements to make sure it is at the right height.

According to Henry Bridenbecker, the jig can be a problem with respect to the notches cut into the jig. Remember, the notch must be cut to the proper bevel of the inside of the frames. With the midship frames, this is not much of a problem, but when you come to the outside frames and the cant frames, you really have a bevel to cut. Henry found that he had a tendency to cut these bevels a little too deep. They would still hold the frame in place, but when the time came to put the wale on—which is the first thing you plank and which holds the model together when you have done so—some of the frames had a tendency to move a little.

To avoid this problem, cut small pieces of ¼-inch wood and glue them right over the platform right behind the frame to make sure it is fit in its proper place. Test every frame in this way prior to the planking process, starting by pushing on each frame to make sure it does not move from its proper place. Even ¹⁄₃₂ inch can throw you off in this process, so make sure all your frames are absolutely true and secure.

Make the jig itself out of a good-quality type of plywood, such as cabinetmaker's plywood. I have found that a poor grade of plywood does not work well at all since the notches cut in the wood tend to break at just the wrong time. The thicker the plywood, the more work you have to do in cutting out the notches. The best choice is a good five-ply birch cabinetmaker's veneer.

Another use for this jig is as a wonderful reference point for building the rest of your model. This jig represents one of the waterlines off of your plans. Be sure to mark this jig surface on each of your frames before you remove the jig prior to planking and after putting in your wales. The reference point this provides to make measurements from your plans

up or down from this waterline will prove to be very valuable, and you will know that this is a very accurate and reliable reference point on your model. This is one reason for choosing the waterline just above your deck for the jig position.

Now you can accurately measure the position of your deck-beam shelf, which will support your deck beams. If you have reached the level of scratch builder, I am assuming you already know that the deck on wooden ships is not a level structure, but is curved both in the fore and aft direction and port and starboard. The *camber,* or curve, of the deck port and starboard can be treated with the proper curve installed as part of the beam. Carefully measure and install the fore and aft curve as part of the beam shelf, which is a plank installed inside the frames fore and aft to support the deck beams.

You will also see at this point that the bevel of the frames on the inside is just as important as the bevel of the frames on the outside. The procedures for building the deck beams, or frames for the deck, is just as important as those for the ship's frames. You can install the deck beams before or after you complete the planking on the outside frames of the ship. If you intend to plank the inside of your frames, as was done on the real ship, then of course you must plank the inside first before putting in the deck beams.

You can also use the jig concept to great advantage if you are a kit builder of a plank-on-bulkhead ship model. When putting your frames up, mark them with a point showing the location of the waterline nearest the deck level. This deck level should be the upper deck level if you are building a large model like a three decker. When building a large model, it will not hurt to mark in a second deck level also.

If the plans do not show a waterline level, draw one in on the ship's plan yourself. This is not a waste of time since you can use this line in several ways. It enables you to make sure that your frames are lined up properly on the keel prior to fastening the frames to your keel. A glance along the ship's length from fore to aft then from aft to fore will reveal a straight line the length of the ship where you have marked the bulkheads. This line also will serve as the reference point for the rest of the hull construction.

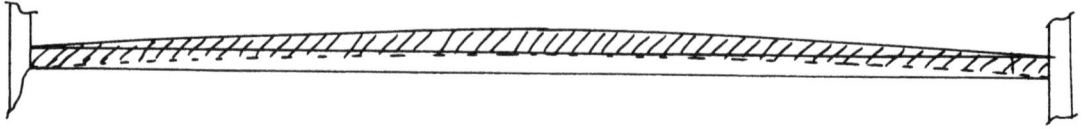

Fig. 2-19. An example of the curve of the deck beam or the camber of the deck.

Proper location of the gunports, particularly on a large ship of the line, can be a real problem if you do not have some point of reference to guide you in finding the right locations. It also is a great help to locate your gunports prior to putting on the first layer of planks and "frame" them like a picture frame with extra wood strips either purchased from a local hobby shop or cut by yourself. An added note is that all wooden plank-on-bulkhead model kits have very little spare wood, if any. If you are going to add details to a ship model kit, you must supply additional wood from some other source.

LOCATION OF THE FALSE DECK

The location of the false deck supplied in kits is also of great importance. One of the pitfalls of wooden ship model kits is the location of this false deck in relation to the sides of the ship or bulkheads. There is a camber to the deck. This camber is the port and starboard curve the deck has from the center of the deck (FIG. 2-19). The line drawn on the bulkheads will help you locate this camber line from the plans and will save you a lot of trouble later, such as when you want to install your cannon on the deck only to find that they do not fit through the gunports because the deck at that point is too high. The only solution to this problem once it exists is to cut down the wheels on the gun carriage or remove the entire deck of the model and start over. So, a little care at the beginning will save you a lot of trouble in the future.

The waterline reference point is a very important part of the ship modeler's construction methods and should not be ignored. You should do anything you can to help in the construction process since the model is difficult enough to build if done right and is much harder to build when there is no reference point from which to make measurements.

FITTING THE PARTS

After you have finished the jig, the frames, and the keel structure, along with the baseboard on which you will work, you can fit the parts together. Place the keel skeleton on the baseboard, put the jig in place, and fit the midship's section frame to the keel. Be sure that the mortice cut into the frame is a good fit, with the keel in its proper location, and also that it fits the notches in the keel. Then, glue the frame to the keel, set in the jig, and let it dry.

At this point, you can admire the work by observing the fine appearance of the single frame set into the keel. Continue to add frames to the keel until all of your square frames are installed.

This leaves you with the cant frames to install. This is where the deadwood you installed earlier comes in to good use. As stated earlier in this chapter, the cant frames are half frames that are "bent" to meet the curve of the planking at the bow and stern of the ship. Grooves for fitting the cant frames must have been carved into the deadwood at the bow, as shown in FIG. 2-20.

Keelson

Before you begin to put in the cant frames, install the *keelson*. This timber is a piece of wood that is laid over the frames and the keel as shown in FIG. 2-21. In real ship building, the keelson could be as much as two or three pieces of timber. Along with the keelson went the inner planking, or *ceiling*, of the ship, which refers to both the "floor" of the hull, as well as the "walls." This inner layer of planking was just like the outer layer of planking and was a lot thicker at the bottom than the sides.

The addition of the ceiling to the inner section of the hull is up to the individual modeler. You should, however, install the keelson in any case since it is

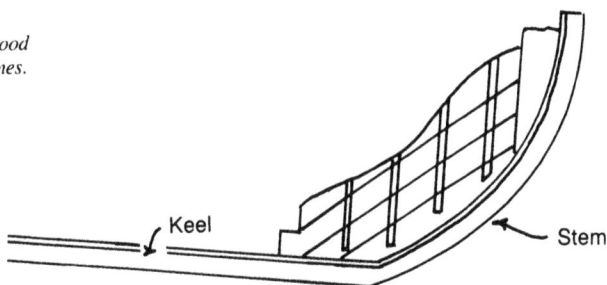

Fig. 2-20. (right) The stem and keel at the bow, with the deadwood in place and the notches cut into the deadwood for the cant frames.

Keel

Stem

Fig. 2-21 (below) A cross section of the keel, frames, and keelson. The keelson goes over the frames and attaches to the keel through the frames by being glued and doweled.

Keelson

Frames →

Keel

the real backbone of the ship model, as it was the real ship, and holds all of the frames firmly together at their base. Before you install the keelson, you must install pieces of wood between the frames to make a solid landing for the keelson.

Once the keelson has been fitted, it is best to dowel it into place to make sure it will not come adrift. Work from the midship's frames toward the bow and stern alternately. Use care to ensure that the dowels are of the proper length, that you do not dowel the keel to the baseboard on which it is setting, and that you cut off the excess part of the dowel above the keelson. Use your pin-vise drill or power drill carefully, marking the depth of the hole to be drilled on the drill with a piece of masking tape or some other device to ensure that you drill the holes the correct depth, and also marking your dowel with a pencil to indicate the proper length so that you can tell when the dowel is in the hole to its proper length. Finish by doweling the keelson into the deadwood at both ends of the ship.

Bulkheads

You also can dowel the plank-on-bulkhead kit model bulkheads to the keel of the model by drilling holes through the bulkhead base and the keel, and back out the other side of the bulkhead base at a slight angle. Then insert a dowel. This procedure might seem like a wasted effort, but it will prevent a bulkhead

from coming loose at a later stage of construction, which could prove to be disastrous.

Cant Frames

You are ready to install the cant frames. Check to make sure there is enough deadwood to dowel the cant frame to. If there is any question, install a bracing across the cant frame to the cant frame on the other side and install them both together just like the previous frames (FIG. 2-22).

Once again, transfer the waterline mark you made on your drawing to the frame, and use this in turn to help make sure that you get the cant frame in its proper location. It will also help, as Henry Bridenbecker says, to make proper templates to assist you in locating the proper angle of cut for the frame prior to installation on the deadwood. Both the port and starboard frame should be at the same position in relationship to one another and at the same height. They should also fit into the jig properly, with the line on the jig matching the waterline on the frame.

With kit models, cant frames are usually ignored. In their place something must be installed to ensure the proper curve at the bow and stern. Good kits at least supply you with filler wood to place in the bow area (FIG. 2-23). Unfortunately, many times this wood filler is balsa wood, which is no good for this purpose.

Substitute another wood from your own supply

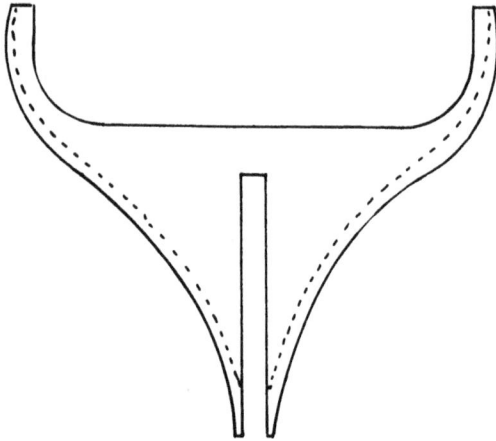

Fig. 2-22. This is a substitute for the cant frames. The dotted line indicates the sharp bevel cut required with this type of substitution. It is similar to the bulkheads furnished in kit models.

of woods. An excellent substitute is to use basswood, but any soft wood can be used as long as it will hold its shape and take nails and a little pressure without losing its shape.

When using filler wood, do not stop at just the bow and stern, but include the spaces between the bulkheads at the keel location. FIGURE 2-23 also indicates the rabbet, which you should cut prior to installing the bulkheads.

Knightheads

If basswood is used for the bow filler, you can also add the *knightheads* to the model. They are the two timbers either side of the stem that rise above the deck. You might need to make some modification of the kit's plans and the false deck if you desire to make the knightheads in this manner. This procedure will result in a much stronger structure then just installing two timbers into the false deck.

You do not have to adhere to the kit plans if you want to improve your model by adding more detail to it. If you do decide to add detail, just make sure that what you are adding is really on the actual ship or at least could have been by the construction standards of the time and country. It does not hurt and can help a great deal if you try to find additional material on the ship you are building. An added help will be some of the books indicated at the end of this book.

If you are a scratch builder, you must add your knightheads while you are installing your frames. You can determine the shape of the knightheads from the ship's plans much the same way you did the shape of the frames.

Also, install the filler pieces between the frames and keel much the same as shown in FIG. 2-23, for the bow area cant frames at least. Any area that can

Fig. 2-23. My model of the Speedy ready for planking. This is a scratch model using some of the kit model methods. Notice the wood filler at the bow area. This type of model will be fully planked.

be improved by adding some extra wood where it will not be seen later is not wasted time.

Batten

You now can place a batten along the run of your frames, and the batten should make good, solid contact with all of your frames. A batten is a piece of wood, say ⅛ × ⅛ inch, which is long enough to run the entire length of your model ship (FIG. 2-24). This is the acid test to see if you have made all of your frames correctly with the right bevel. If the batten does not run from bow to stern cleanly and smoothly while making good contact with all of your frames, then you have not done your frames in the correct way or you have made a measurement error.

At this stage of the model, it is almost impossible to correct this type of problem. If the frame is too large, which means the frame bevel was not cut enough and not enough wood was removed, then removing this wood is not that difficult to do. If you have a hollow, then you have removed too much wood and you can correct it by adding wood as is done with the kit type plank-on-bulkhead model.

The ideal is to not have to resort to these methods, but to have come out with a clean set of frames, which shows that your measurements and craftsmanship are of the best. This is one of the results of being satisfied with only the best you can possibly do, and not with something that will just get by. Accurately doing the job is the way fine ship models are built.

Wale

Next you install your wale. First, however, there is another important item to take care of. Your jig, which holds your frames in place, must be absolutely rigid. Again check all of your frames to make sure none of them has a tendency to move even a little bit. You do not want to have one side of your ship higher than the other because you did not make sure your frames were equal and firm before you secured them. You have already placed wooden ''blocks'' against each frame to make sure it does not move (FIG. 2-25).

The *wale* of your ship is the item that will hold your ship together and enable you to remove your jig. One final item must be checked before you install your

the wale: the band of wood at the midship's section of your hull that is generally thicker than the rest of your planking. The jig holding the frames in position must not extend beyond the surface of the frames. The slots that hold the frames must be only as deep as the thickness of the frame.

Glue and dowel the wale right where the jig is located for maximum strength. Also, do not forget to locate your reference waterline mark where you can see it after the wale has been installed.

Deck Beams and Braces

You can install your deck beams and braces internally, before you install your wale. You must remove your jig to do this. I prefer to install the wale first, then do the planking, then install my deck beams and internal structure, since I already have a jig that will hold my frames firmly in place and will have a solid structure once my wales are installed port and starboard.

ANOTHER FRAMING METHOD

This is not the only way to frame the scratch-built plank-on-frame model. There are other ways of doing the frames, one of which is shown in FIG. 2-26. This method of construction is different from the method described previously in this chapter.

These frames must be constructed on a flat surface, preferably a strong piece of glass, such as the piece used for the construction of the keel assembly. You start with the midship frame again, but this time all of the frames will come in contact with each other. For the midship frame, use seven parts of the frame to make up one whole, as shown in the way that the frames are put together. The result is that one entire band of wood runs the length of the hull. Thus, you can dowel all of the frames together (FIGS. 2-27 and 2-28). This is the method, or at least appears to be the method, the modelers of the eighteenth century used to make all of those beautiful Admiralty models that many wooden ship modelers want to produce some day.

I have not used this framing method, but several of the modelers in the Ship Modelers Association of Fullerton, California have used this method with

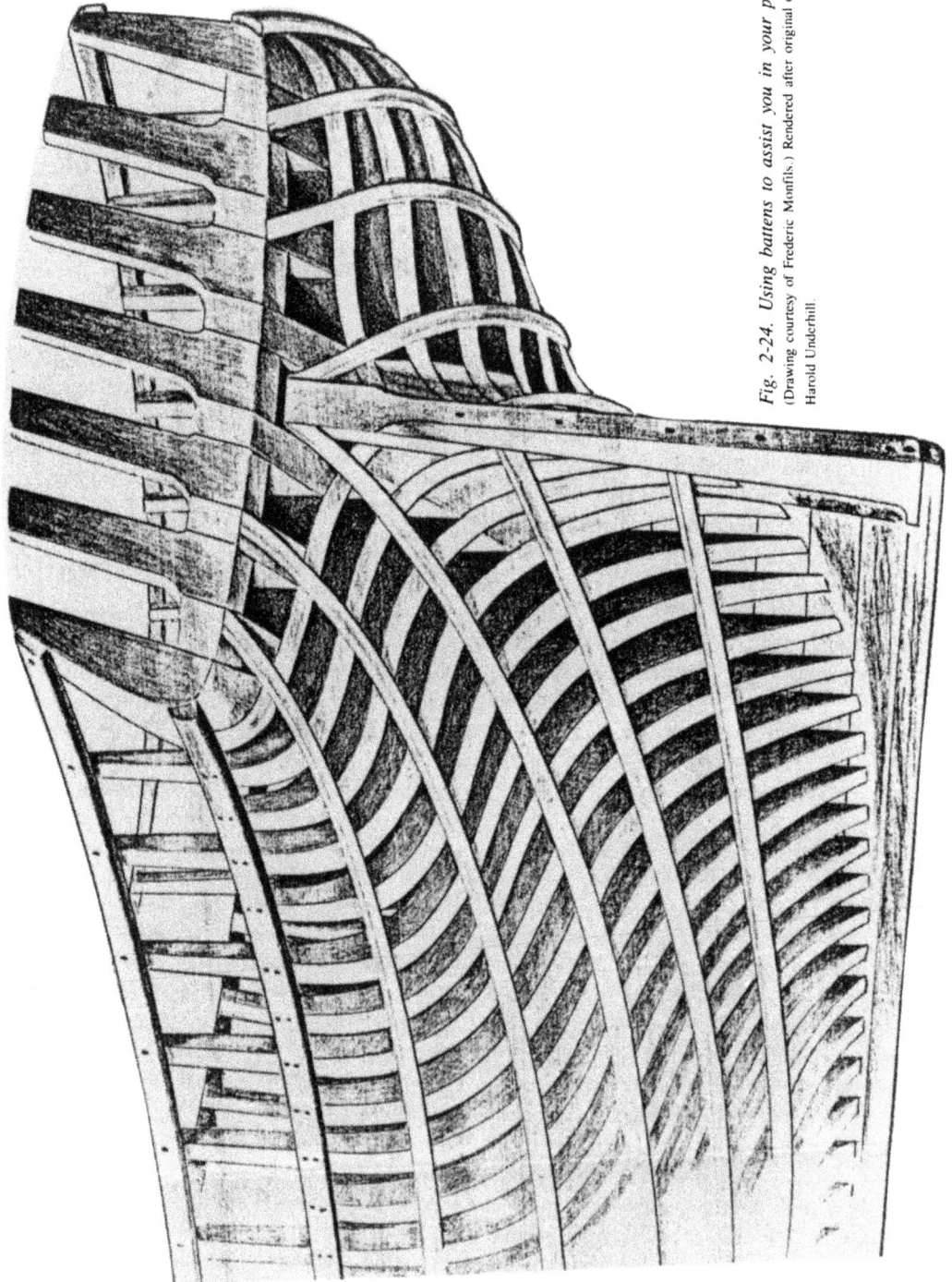

Fig. 2-24. Using battens to assist you in your planking. (Drawing courtesy of Frederic Monfils.) Rendered after original drawing by Harold Underhill.

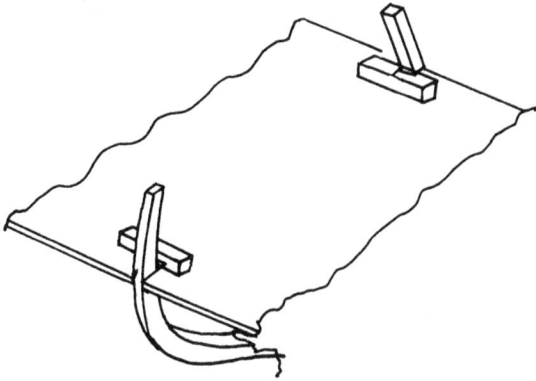

Fig. 2-25. *An example of the blocks in place glued onto the framing jig to make sure the frames do not move when you begin to plank your model.*

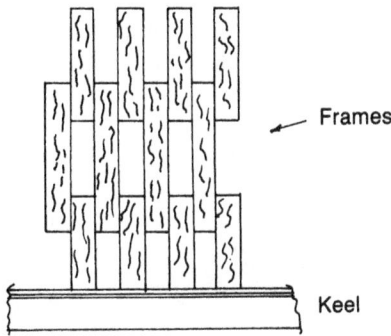

Frames

Keel

Fig. 2-26. *Another method of construction of the frames for your plank-on-frame model. This method is sometimes referred to as the* admiralty *method.*

excellent results. The all-important frame jig is used with this method of construction also. I do not know of any method of building a plank-on-frame ship model that does not use some form of the frame jig.

Once the midship frame is constructed, install it on the keel, which you should make very much like that described earlier. Also, you will again need to make drawings, with the patterns of the frames drawn out very much like what was described before.

The frames are composed of five parts with the exception of the midship frame, which is made up of seven parts. You must make all of these frames with as much attention to detail and scale as was done with the other method of frame construction. One point here is that all of the frames must be of the same

thickness. Again, if the frames vary in thickness, then your ship will be longer or shorter than it should be, depending on where you make your mistake.

The parts of the frame are the floor, or bottom of the frame that fits onto the keel; the two top timbers, which are the port and starboard top parts of the frame; and the middle part of the frame, port and starboard, which is called the *futtock*. The midship frame has futtock pieces both fore and aft of its top timbers and floor timber, since it is the middle frame of the hull. FIGURE 2-28 shows completed frames; FIG. 2-29 shows Ed Marple's frames under construction for his ship model the *Conqueror*.

Make a pattern of each frame and lay it out on the piece of glass. Glue the floor timber and the two top timbers of the midship frame to the paper pattern using rubber cement. Be sure that the wood pieces are glued true to the pattern. Then with your wood cement, glue the futtocks port and starboard onto the floor and top timbers, thus joining them. Again, be sure to follow the drawn pattern on the paper. Put a weight on this structure and let it set.

After it has set, turn the frame over and brace the floor and the top timbers with some spare wood the same thickness as the rest of your frame material. With wood glue, fix the other futtocks port and starboard to the midship floor and top timbers. Remove the paper pattern before you glue on the second set of futtocks.

You have now finished your first frame and all of the other frames will follow the same procedure, except you will only have one set of futtocks to install. Again, dowel all parts to each other. You can dowel each set of frames to the already installed frame on the keel before moving on to the next frame. You can install each frame as it is constructed.

HELPS

One group of items that can save you much time, not only with this method of construction but all items discussed in this text, are cardboard templates. Use them to fit a part before you actually cut the part out of a piece of wood. This will not only save you a lot of wood, but will also save you a lot of time in the long run.

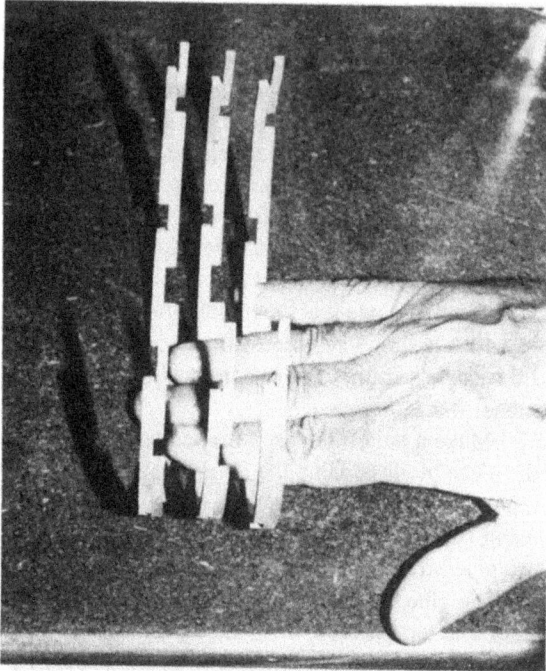

Fig. 2-27. A view of Bob Saddoris' frames for his model of the Mayflower. Bob said this is the way the Mayflower's frames were built.

Unless you are an exceptionally skilled craftsman, making something as complex as a frame out of several pieces of wood requires patterns and drawn plans. Also, even the most skilled craftsman can make a mistake. Do not make the mistake of keeping a part that you spent a lot of time on but is not quite right. If you can do better, then do so. This is a hobby for most people, so there are no timetables and no deadlines to meet in order to complete the model. You can afford to discard something and do it over, if for no other reason than your own satisfaction.

RESEARCH AND OTHER METHODS

There are other methods used by modelers to make frames, in addition to those indicated previously. All methods of making frames do require a minimum of a good set of plans. FIGURE 2-30 shows a type of bulkhead frame where the lower portion of the frame is a bulkhead with a hole cut in it for the keelson. The upper portion of the unit is the top timber of the conventional frame.

Some modelers have made their frames out of one piece of wood. If you use a one-piece frame, you will need to make sure the wood is very well seasoned,

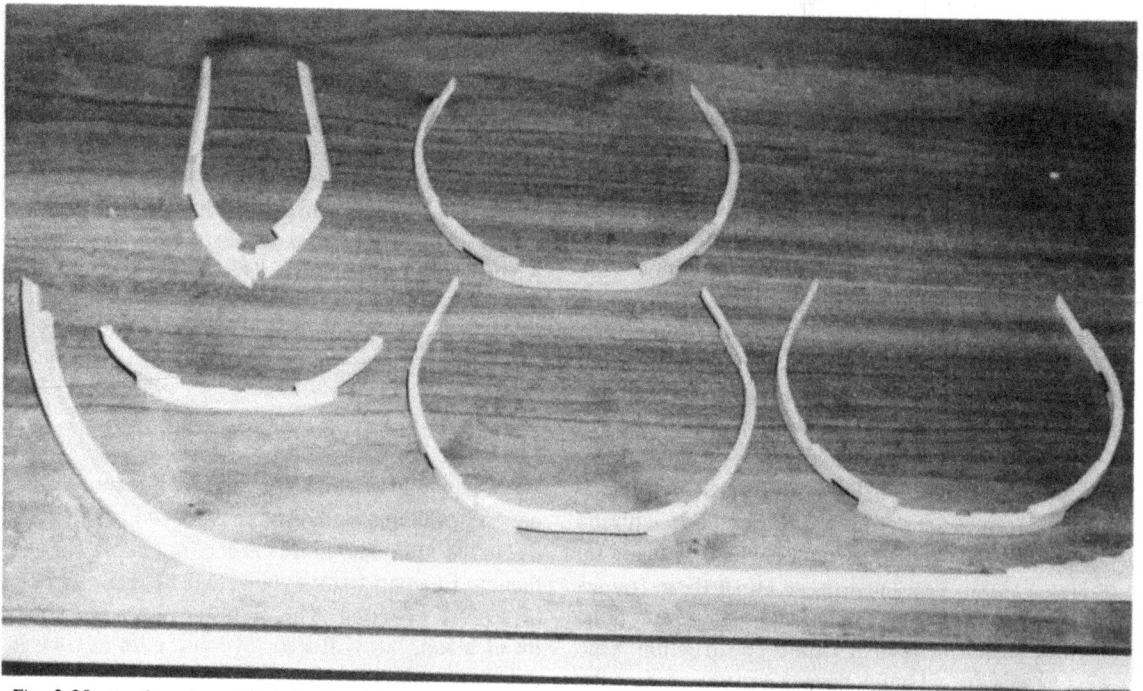

Fig. 2-28. Another view of Bob Saddoris' frames of the Mayflower.

that the grain is such that the wood will be strong enough to stand up when it is cut out, and that the frames are again properly spaced. This spacing is especially important when your model has gunports.

Some modelers go to the extent of building the ship like the real thing was built. This is the ultimate in ship modeling. FIGURE 2-31 shows all of the frames as was done in a real ship. The side view shows you the basic construction of the hull of a warship and how much wood was used in the construction. War ships were always built heavier than merchant ships, so the frame spacing of a merchant ship might have not been as close as a warship, depending on its intended use. The best guide is again the plans.

Again, if you are using a kit, you might want to invest a little time researching your model and trying to obtain another set of plans of the same ship from a museum. Some of the museums that I have corresponded with are listed in the back of this book. All of the museums have been very cooperative and helped in every way they can, so they are always your primary source for plans. The Nautical Research Guild is also listed, along with several hobby shops I have dealt with and obtained plans from.

The kit modeler should be warned that there are kit models available, which are apparently made up by the manufacturer (I could not find any additional plans from any other source). As an example, I purchased the kit model of the *Le Mirage* by Corel of Italy, which is a plank-on-bulkhead type model kit. The kit itself was a good kit as kits go in that most of the material supplied was usable and the plans were well done as far as they went. As usual, there were no details on the planking, so I added it. After I had already began construction, however, I sent a request to several museums in France asking about the history of this ship and if there were any museum plans available of her. All of my replies indicated that as far as the museum could tell there was never a ship of this name in the French Navy during the reign of Louis XIV, as claimed by Corel. I built the model as planned by Corel and it is a good-looking model of a typical ship of the period, but it cannot be authenticated.

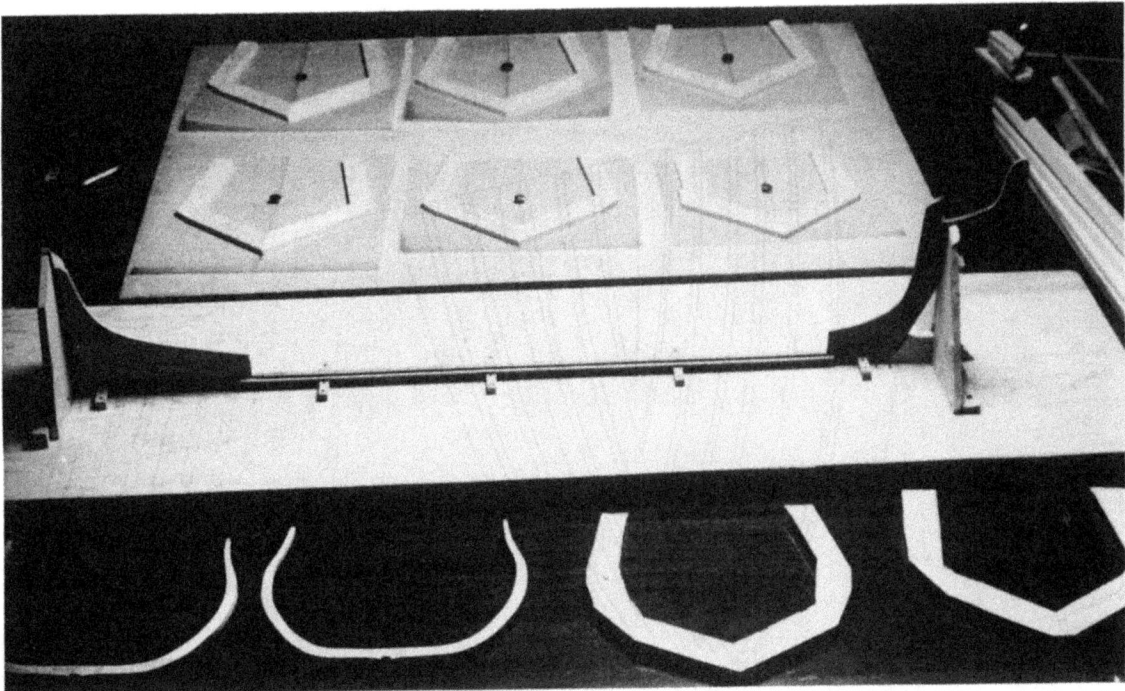

Fig. 2-29. A picture of the frames of Ed Marple's Conqueror under construction. This picture indicates how the frames are made, gluing the wood parts together and doweling, then cutting the frames out to shape. The lines of the soon to be cut out frame can be seen on the lower right side of the photograph. (Photo courtesy of Ed Marple.)

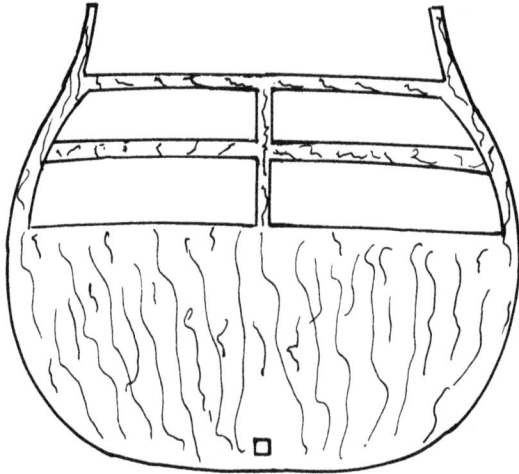

Fig. 2-30. A view of another type of scratch frame. Notice the hole cut in the bottom of the frame for the keelson.

On the positive side, many kit models are available that can be authenticated by plans from museums and other sources. It is also possible that I did not go far enough in my research of the *Le Mirage,* and perhaps I will find out more information as a result of this book. FIGURE 2-32 pictures my model of *Le Mirage.* The rigging is not kit but scratch, but the hull is essentially kit.

One method of making a solid hull I have already mentioned is the bread-and-butter method, using several layers of wood. Many modelers scratch-build using this method over the plank-on-frame or plank-on-bulkhead methods with excellent results. This is the same method used by solid-hull kit manufacturers in making their solid-hull shapes in rough. If you are a beginner, you might want to start out with this type of kit model to have a firm surface for your first

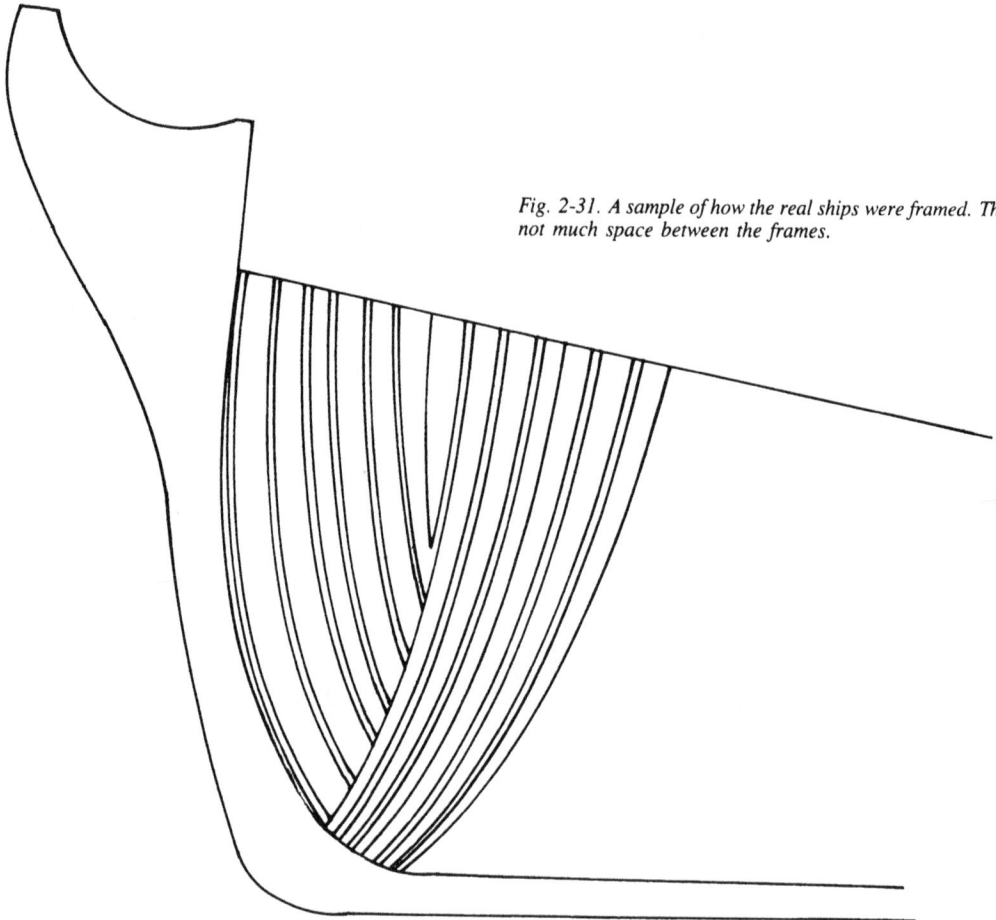

Fig. 2-31. A sample of how the real ships were framed. There was not much space between the frames.

planking effort, but I have seen beginners start out with plank-on-bulkhead kits with excellent results.

Another method of frame construction that has been used by members of the Ship Modelers Association of Fullerton (S.M.A.) is the one invented by Harold Hahn. Mr. Hahn's book is listed in the back of this text, along with all of the other books on the subject of planking that I am aware of. Bill Wicks, a member of the ship club, has used Mr. Hahn's method and says he thinks it is one of the best methods he has found to build a plank-on-frame ship. (See FIG. 2-33.)

One of the big advantages of using this method is that the frames are already drawn out for you by Mr. Hahn, if you obtain the plans from him. His book describes and illustrates his method of frame construction with his use of the framing jig. His models are framed upside down, with extra long frames that are later cut to the proper size.

S.M.A. MEMBERS' METHODS

Another method used by a member of the S.M.A. is to make a mold of the entire ship model out of sol-id wood formed to the lines of the inside layer of planking of the hull. He cut the mold into various shapes so he could remove it once the model was planked. He pinned the mold together, waxed it, and then installed the inner layer of planking. He then installed the frames onto the inner layer of planking, staggering the frames and planking to allow the entire model to be taken apart like a jig saw puzzle. Next, he applied the outer layer of planking. When the entire model was built in this way, he took it apart to remove the inner mold. This process included the decks of the ship as he went. The decks were sandwiched in between the molds at each level. In this way, Howard Judson built a model of the *Half Moon*. The wood Howard used was basswood planking and hardwood mold. It was a highlight of one of our club meetings to see Howard take apart and put back together his model of the *Half Moon*.

Paul Greenlee, a member of the S. M. A., developed his own method of making frames by forming the hull out of many sections of wood cut the thickness of a frame, and gluing the entire hull together to form one solid hull. Next, he finished the hull shape on

Fig. 2-32. My kit model of Corel's Le Mirage *with many rigging modifications. The model was rigged using Anderson's book as a reference guide.*

the outside, much like a conventional wooden hull. He then soaked the parts apart and removed every other piece of wood, thus leaving him with bulkheads. He then cut out the interior shape, leaving him with his frames, which he glued to his stem, keel, and sternpost. FIGURE 2-34 is the result of this method of construction.

Rolly Kalajian, another S.M.A. member, is a retired ship builder who decided he would like to build a model of the ship he once built himself. He is following the actual practice he used when he built the real thing. He built the frames for his ship using a mold for each frame, the frame itself being laminated out of many layers of thin wood. He then released the mold and beveled the frame as required. He made two frames at the same time and then cut the laminated "double frame" in half to give him two frames. He made the frames thicker than necessary to make sure there would be enough wood left to cut the bevel onto the frames. Rolly designed and built the real ship in 1951 in San Pedro, California, and is building the model to the scale of ¾ inch. FIGURE 2-35 is a picture of his model under construction, showing his frames as installed.

This is also Rolly's first ship model, which shows that the beginner can build a fine-scale ship model if he follows the actual practice of the real builder as closely as he can. Rolly does have an advantage here, but I have seen other modelers who have built fine, "museum-quality" ship models with their first or second effort. It can be done. Also, many of the models mentioned in the text are pictured in this book. I only hope that you can see the detail of the frame structure and planking methods indicated.

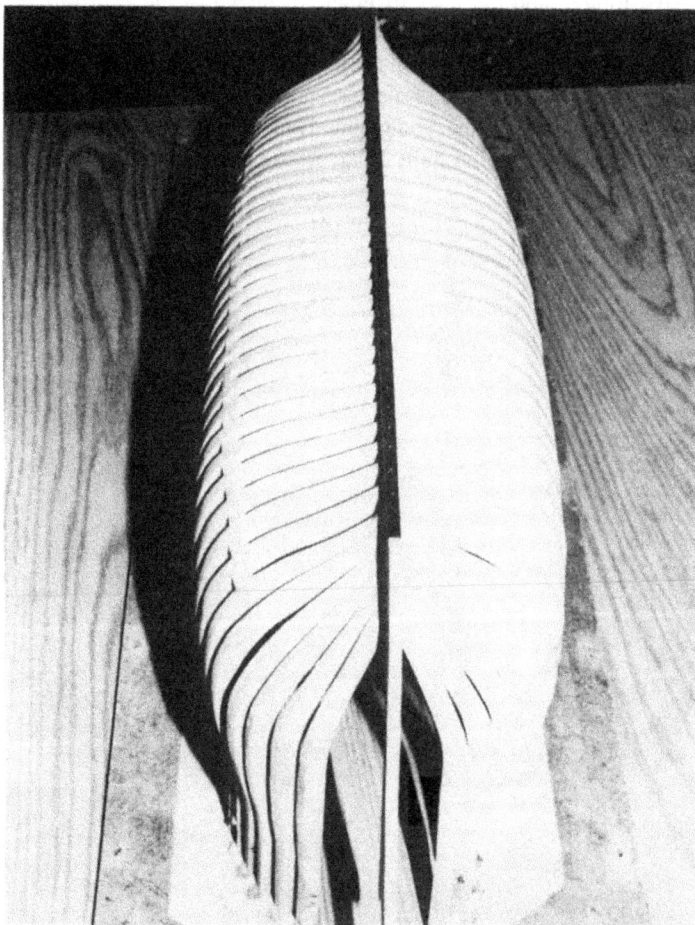

Fig. 2-33. Bill Wicks' model under construction using Harold Hahn's method of construction. The plans of the H.M.S. Druid were obtained from Mr. Hahn.

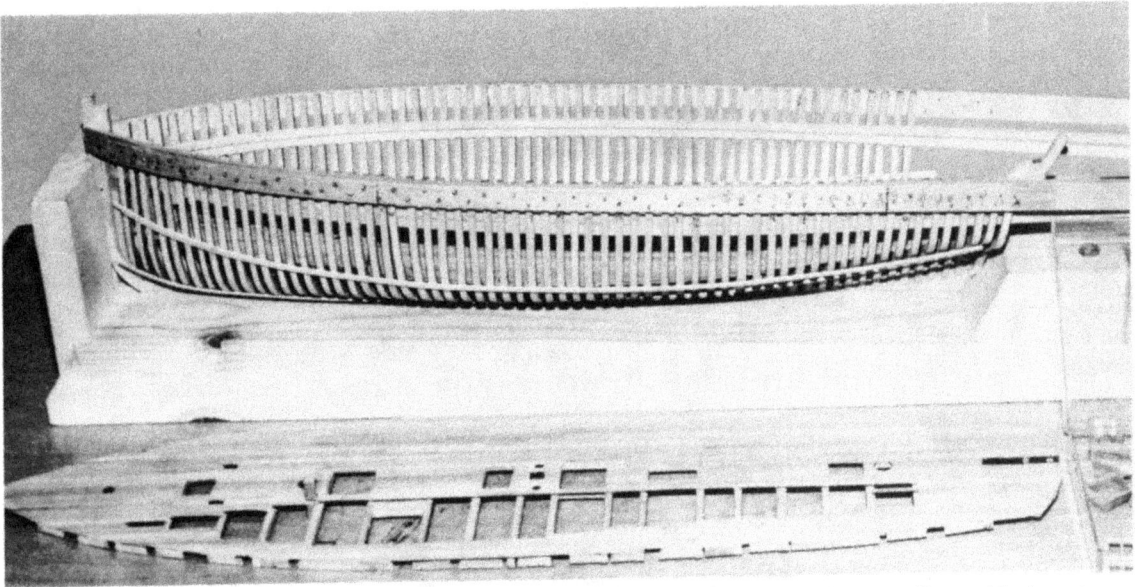

Fig. 2-34. Paul Greenlee's model under construction using yet another method of making the frames as discussed in the text.

Fig. 2-35. A model built by Rolly Kalajian of a ship he built himself. The White Wings II features yet another method to make the frames since he laminated them together.

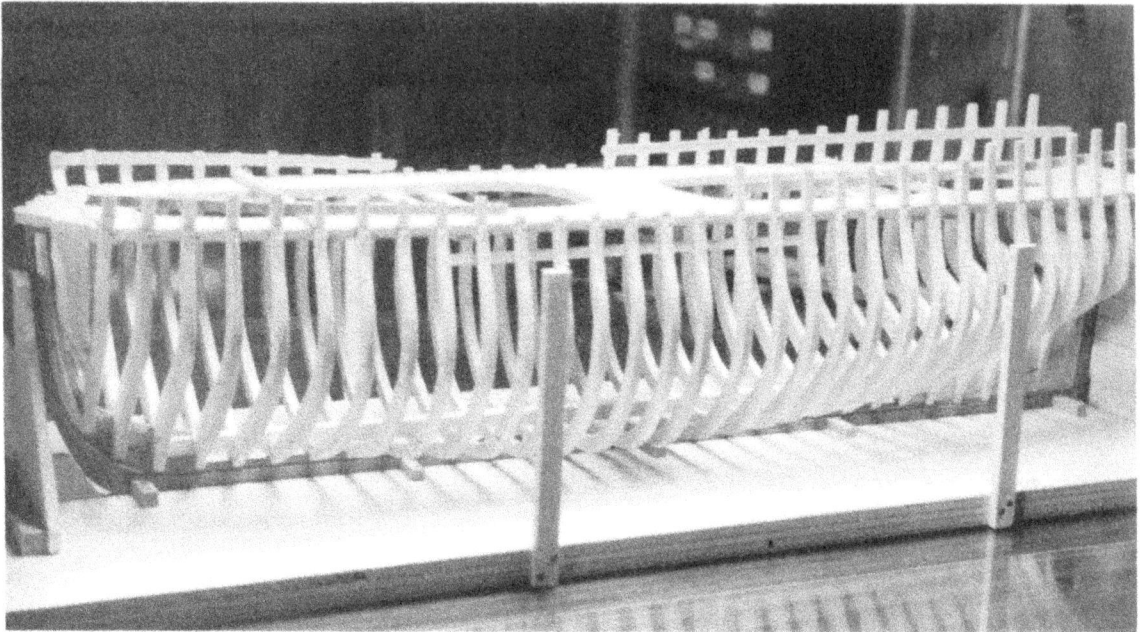

Fig. 2-36. Another view of the framing of Conqueror. *This gives a good view of the framing jig and the building board.* (Photo courtesy of Ed Marple.)

Fig. 2-37. A view of another one of Ed Marple's ships in the frame stage. This one is the Sovereign of the Seas. *Notice the batten in place.* (Photo courtesy of Ed Marple.)

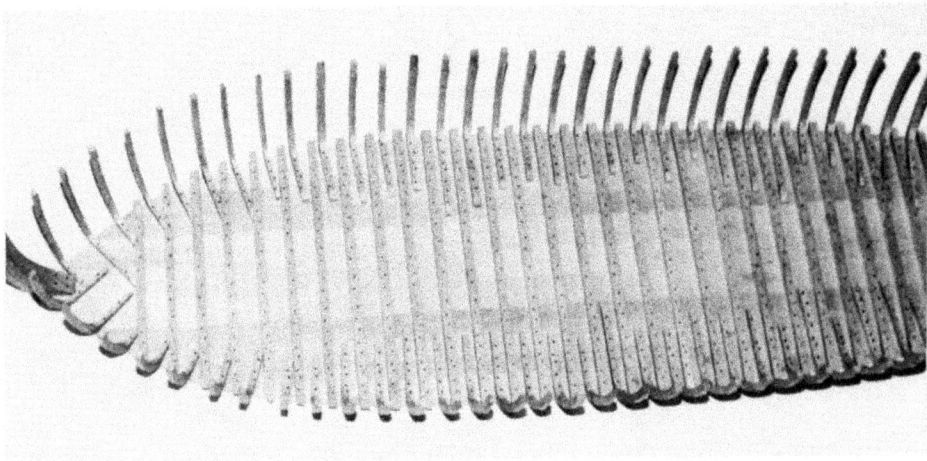

Fig. 2-38. A model by Dave Yotter of the Philadelphia *gondola gun boat ready for planking.*

The frames of the model having been completed, and the stern of the model having been resolved, you can go to the next chapter, which deals with planking.

FIGURES 2-36 through 2-38 show different ships in the final stages of framing on their building boards and ready for planking.

3

Planking The Ship's Hull

THE FIRST ORDER OF PLANKING IS TO MAKE SURE your frames are rigidly supported or, in the case of the kit-type bulkhead model, that your bulkheads are rigid. If there are any gunports, you should locate them before you begin any planking. If you have done all procedures outlined in the previous chapter, then you are ready to plank.

SOLID-HULL PLANKING

Planking of a solid hull is one of the best ways of being introduced to the art of planking, because you have a solid surface to plank and do not need to worry about hollows and bumps in your planking, assuming that the solid-hull blank is properly finished with no faults in the smooth flow of the hull lines. *Planking* is installing wooden strips of wood to the hull to cover the frames, much like building the walls of a house once the frame has been constructed. Solid-hull models give you a solid frame to work from. It will help if you have cut a rabbet into your solid hull between the hull and the keel, stem, and sternpost. This will provide a notch to install the ends of your planks, and a smooth surface between the keel structure and the hull.

Since it is best to follow actual shipbuilding practice to obtain the best results, the first plank you will install is the wale plank at deck level. You are at a crossroads almost right away in your planking process. You need to decide if you are going to plank the model with strips of wood the entire length of the model, or cut strips of wood to the proper size to make up the full length of the model.

In real life, you would not be able to find a length of wood 60 feet, and even if you did, it would be quite difficult to work with when planking a hull. The general rule is that planks were actually about 30 feet long at their maximum, so you can work from there, converting 30 feet into the proper length of wood strip to the scale you are using. If you have chosen to plank the ship with no regard for the length of the strip, then you do not need to make these calculations.

Having a solid-hull kit you will not have any planks supplied in the kit. You must either find a source of the planks already cut (several of which are listed in the back of this book), or cut your own. The choice of wood has already been discussed in Chapter 1, so you will now need to decide on the method of cutting to use and the size to cut the wood of your choice. If you opt to buy the wood already cut into strips, then a letter to the proper source identifying the wood of your choice and the size of cut desired will accomplish your goal, but it can get expensive, especially if you opt for boxwood, pearwood, or some other rare wood.

Assuming you do not want to pay the high cost of already cut wood, then you will need to be able to cut your own stock. You can purchase a miniature table saw, of which several are available at your local hobby shop, such as the Dremel, or the Unimat tool with the saw attachment. I have used both and find that the better the saw, the better the results you get. Also, the use of a fine-tooth saw is a must.

Another choice is to make your own table saw. A saw of this type was made by one of the members of the S.M.A. It consisted of a ⅜-inch drill laid on its side, and a mandrel installed into the chuck of the drill, with a small slitting saw blade attached. The drill was secured to a wooden base and a wooden table was made to fit over the mandrel of the drill with a slit in it to accommodate the saw blade. The little wooden table had a miter gauge on it, along with the other accessories normally included with a table saw. It was raised and lowered by raising and lowering the tabletop itself. This saw seemed to work very well. The stock it turned out was just as good as the stock I turned out on my Unimat.

If you opt to buy a power tool such as a miniature saw, I strongly recommend the Unimat tool. It can do so many things other than working as a table saw. It is basically a lathe, and can be used as a wood lathe also. It also has attachments to make it a miniature planer of wood, a jigsaw, and other things such as a disk sander.

Having made your wood selection, the next step is to install your wale. The wale is the extra-thick plank that goes around your hull, usually at the widest point of the hull. Larger ships have more than one wale, so the main wale will be your first plank in this case.

Carefully mark out the location of the main wale on the solid hull from the plans. Be sure to follow the sheer or curve of this timber. FIGURE 3-1 shows a wale cross section. It is apparent that this timber is thicker than the rest of your planking. Obtain the thickness of all of your planks from your plans.

You can cut out these wale planks using your saw. Plan the piece of wood first to the wale thickness desired, then cut the strips out. Cut yourself a little extra wood just in case you should make a mistake. It is a pain to have to go back later and set up the

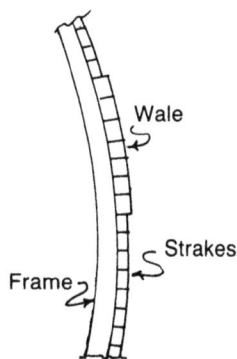

Fig. 3-1. The thickness of the wood used on the ship's hull was not always the same. The wale is much thicker than the strakes or planks of the hull.

saw again just to finish a small piece of wood. At this time, you can also cut the rest of your planking, since you already have your table set up. Again, cut yourself some extra stock since there will be some waste as you plank the hull.

PLANK-ON-BULKHEAD HULL

I will now go to the plank-on-bulkhead kit model and get the basic items ready for planking the wale on this type of model ship construction before I go into the details of planking. I hope you will read this book in its entirety because the beginner has much to learn and can gain a lot by seeing how all modelers work; the middle-of-the-road modeler who builds kits and is on the verge of building his first scratch model can gain experience by using the same methods on one of his kit models; and the scratch builder will perhaps discover a new way of doing the job. Also, there is more than one way of doing the job the right way, as I have discovered. Learning to do something several different ways can be both fun and challenging.

If you are building plank-on-bulkhead kit models, most of which are double-planked, you will need to install your first layer of planks to the hull before you do anything else. The first layer of planks are furnished in the kit, and are usually enough to do the job. If you have built these kit models in the past, do not throw any leftover planking material away. It might come in handy on your next model. If you do not have enough material to finish the hull for some reason, then you should go back to the hobby shop or dealer where you purchased the kit and request some additional wood to complete the first layer of planking.

When planking the first layer on a plank-on-bulkhead kit model, you do not want to position the planks exactly like the second layer of planks. Your first layer of thick planking is meant for hull strength only, since you do not have as many support structures as does the modeler who is framing his ship properly or who has added extra bulkheads to the keel structure, and since the first layer will not be visible when you have completed your second layer of planking.

I am assuming that you have studied your plans carefully and know what you are going to do next. One variation in the usual way of planking kits is to mark out all of your gunports with supports of some kind before you begin to plank your first layer and then plank up to, not over, these gunports, cutting your planks for this purpose (FIG. 3-2). Be sure to follow the mark you have made along your deck line and make all measurements from this line. FIGURE 3-3 shows Ed Marple's method of cutting out gunports after planking the model on his model of the *Conqueror*.

You can use this first layer of planks for practice test procedures in relation to the planking process. This is also the first area in which you will bend your planks. To make the planks very easy to bend, soak the planks in a solution of ammonia and water. They cannot be glued in place while wet, so you must bend them to shape and allow them to dry before you apply them to the hull of the ship model. Therefore, you will need to use one of the jigs for bending planks.

If you are planking a clipper type bow with little curve, you might not need to resort to this bending procedure if the planks can be installed with little or no force exerted on them. With a blunt-bowed ship such as most warships, however, you will have to soak and bend your planks for the bow area at least. In some cases, like for the construction of some Dutch ships, which have rounded sterns as well as rounded bows, you will need to soak both ends of the planks. When planking the first layer, do not try to cut the planks to follow real practice, since this first layer

is mainly for strength. Run the planks from bow to stern in one piece.

FIGURE 1-8 shows one method of bending the bow planks. You can bend them in sets of six to eight in the jig to avoid waiting for long periods of time for the bow planks to dry.

There are other methods of bending the planks than soaking in ammonia and water. The electric plank bender described in Chapter 1 and made by Aeropiccola of Italy has been very helpful to me in bending some very stubborn planks. Also, you can speed up the process of planking by drying the planks faster and bending them over the plank-bending tool while the tool is in a vise or holder. Some modelers do not care for this method of planking, and I have planked ships without using it, but it does come in handy at times.

The candle method also has been used by some modelers with some success, but I usually scorch the wood. With some woods you can actually bend the wood by running it through your thumb and forefinger rapidly. You can also just soak the wood in water with no ammonia. Some of the S.M.A. members do not like the fact that sometimes the wood is discolored by the ammonia when it has been soaked in that solution.

Soaking the wooden planks for your ship in the ammonia and water solution can be hard on the nose since the ammonia is so strong. One way to avoid this is to prepare yourself a 1-inch PVC or plastic pipe cut the length of your planks. Also buy two rubber stoppers or rubber pads, like those used at the ends of a crutch, that will fit the diameter of the plastic tube. Install one rubber stopper at one end of the plastic pipe, fill the pipe with ammonia and water, insert your planks to be soaked, and put the other rubber stopper on the other end. After several hours, remove the planks from this solution and bend them to whatever shape you desire.

One word of caution. I have been told by some members of the S.M.A. that some woods will again become hard if left too long in the solution of ammonia and water, so take care when choosing the wood you are using. I have never had this problem using walnut, pearwood, English sycamore, or boxwood.

Begin your planking by starting at your wale

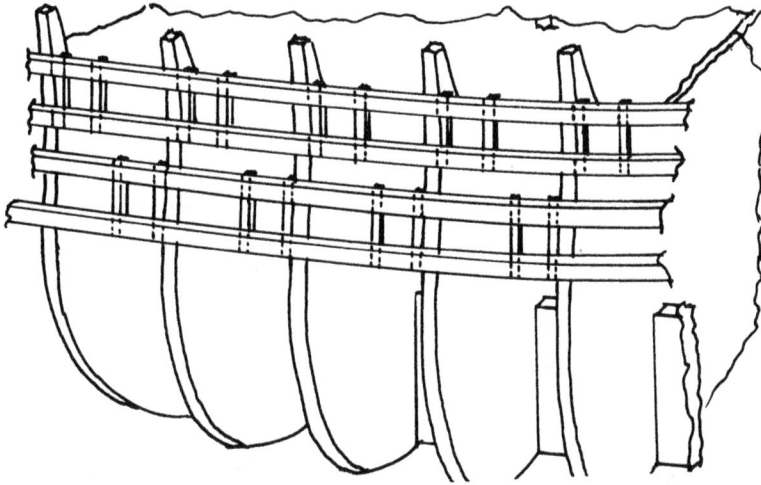

Fig. 3-2. Locate your gunport positions before you begin to plank the hull. This is the way I do my models, including the kit-built models. Some kits have this feature built into them.

Fig. 3-3. Another view of Ed's Conqueror a little further along in construction. All gunports are now cut out. (Photo courtesy of Ed Marple.)

location, first on the port side and then on the starboard side. You will install all of your planks in this same order, first on the port side and then on the starboard side. This method will prevent the hull from being twisted out of shape, which might happen if you plank one side of the ship entirely before you plank the other. This rule applies even for just a few planks. It might not seem like the planks are exerting much force on the frame structure, but they are and it must be balanced on both sides.

At the same time, you should plank from the wale down and from the keel up. In this way, the last plank will be at the turn of the hull about in the middle, and will be one of the easiest to install. Take care not to destroy the rabbet, which you have installed in your keel structure and which must be flush to your final planking. If necessary, cut this rabbet out again using your X-ACTO or Uber knife. Again, be very careful with the rabbet and make it as clean as you can. This procedure is demonstrated on the ship model built by Ed Marple (FIG. 3-4).

After you have installed the first layer of planking, check to make sure that the run of the planking is smooth and free from bumps and hollows. Do sand your model at this point. Make the model ship hull as smooth as you can. If there are bumps, sand them

away. If there are hollows, fill them in with wood filler.

Here is where you will use the sawdust that you saved when you were cutting your planks. You can also use the sawdust obtained from sanding the hull. Mix the sawdust with a little wood glue and make your own wood putty out of the same material as the original wood. This makes the subsequent sanding easier.

Some commercial wood fillers do not sand like the rest of the wood. This problem does not occur with Elmer's Professional Wood Filler, which is used by carpenters and cabinetmakers. It sands just like the wood around the filled area and gives you a nice, flat, smooth finish.

The shape of the planks will vary as you plank your hull. FIGURE 3-5 indicates the change in the shape of the plank as you plank your ship from bow to stern. With the first planking, do the shaping of your planks by eye to avoid duplicating the run of the second layer of planking. To start, take two full planks and sand them with a sanding disk to shape the bow area. The proper way of planking is to use the same number of planks running the entire length of the hull on both sides. This should be true even for the first layer of planks because of the strength factor of this method. FIGURE 3-5 shows a plank being shaped to fit the bow

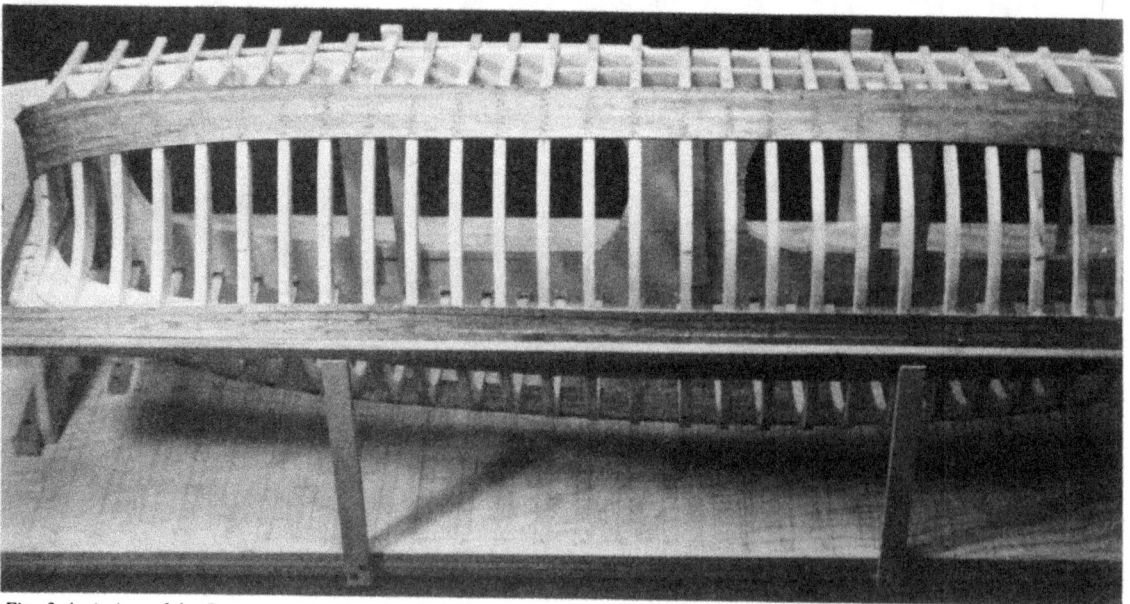

Fig. 3-4. A view of the Conqueror *showing the planks being laid. Notice that the planks from both the bottom up and from the wale* down. (Photo courtesy of Ed Marple.)

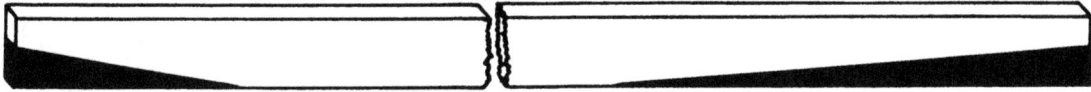

Fig. 3-5. A drawing showing the removal of an unwanted wood at both ends of a plank.

and stern area. Remove some of the wood from the side of the plank, as shown, since the area to cover at the bow is much less than the area at midships.

One special plank that must be discussed at this point is the *garboard strake*. This plank is the first one at the bottom of the ship and intersects the frame and the keel. You must exercise care to ensure that the rabbet is not destroyed when you install this plank with the first layer of planking. Be sure your rabbet is ready for the final layer of planking material. The garboard strake should run the natural length of the ship. Be sure on the first layer of planking that the plank does not have a ridge between it and the keel or rabbet. If there is a ridge, remove it before you begin to install your final planking or it will not fit. FIGURE 3-6 illustrates this ridge and its removal with a knife, file, or sandpaper.

When you are planking the first layer of the model, lay and glue the planks to each other and to the sides of the bulkheads as shown in FIG. 3-7. Remove the unwanted wood resulting from the plank being laid only on one side, as shown in FIG. 3-5. This will leave you with a flat, level surface on one edge of the plank just fixed to your hull, upon which you can place your next plank. FIGURE 3-8 illustrates this concept, which makes it easier to plank.

Both sides of the ship must be symmetrical. Both sides should have the same number of planks and should look the same when viewed from the bow. FIGURE 3-9 shows this aspect off very well, but also shows what should not be done, particularly on the second layer of the planking process. The planks on the lower one-third of the hull were installed or terminated into another plank on the hull, instead of coming all the way to the keel or stem. This is not the correct way to install planking, since, again, the planks must run from the bow to the stem. The only exception to this rule is when steelers are installed (discussed later in this chapter). I do not think ships were ever built in this way since there is no support behind planks installed in this manner. It also destroys the beautiful run of the planking on your ship's hull, which is one of the main objectives of planking the hull.

The planks around the curve of the bilge or side of the ship can be sanded slightly on one edge to give the side of the plank a slightly beveled shape so that when it is glued to the previous plank already on the hull, it will glue more firmly without leaving a gap (FIG. 3-10). This requires only a slight swipe with a sanding block or a file by hand. Power equipment here would remove too much wood.

Completely plank the first layer of your ship model with the first layer of planking. Check the entire ship model for the proper symmetry. You must fill in any hollows, sand away all humps in the hull, and sand the hull to a smooth finish. The kit model's first layer of planking is usually thick, so you can sand quite a bit without too much worry. If you have done a good job in the first place, very little sanding will be needed.

Now is the time to make sure your hull is of the proper shape while you can still do something to correct any problems. Once you start your final planking, there is little you can do to fix the hull. Run a plank along the hull in several different places to see if the run of your first layer of planking is smooth and true. If it is, make sure again that you still have your point of reference along the waterline. This mark is still of great importance because you now will have to locate your wale line. Make sure that the correct sheer or curve of the wale is obtained from your plans. The installation of the wale and the second layer of planking can then follow the same practice as that of the scratch builders with their plank-on-frame ship models.

A method of forming planks to obtain the thicker and thinner parts of the plank is shown in FIG. 3-5. My method is to glue two planks to each other using rubber cement. I draw a line to show the amount of wood to be removed from the two planks. I then sand the two planks on a sanding disk to remove the required amount of wood, following carefully the line

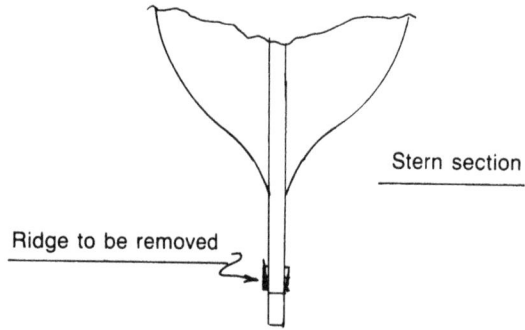

Stern section

Ridge to be removed

Fig. 3-6. The part of the plank that must be sanded away on kit-built models. Be careful you do not ruin your rabbet if you have cut one in for your final planking.

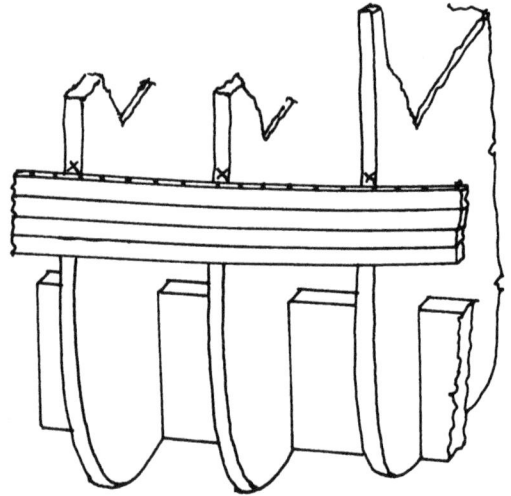

Fig. 3-7. Placing glue on a plank when installing. Glue plank to plank, as well as to the frames. The dashed lines on the plank edges should have glue along with the x marks on the bulkheads.

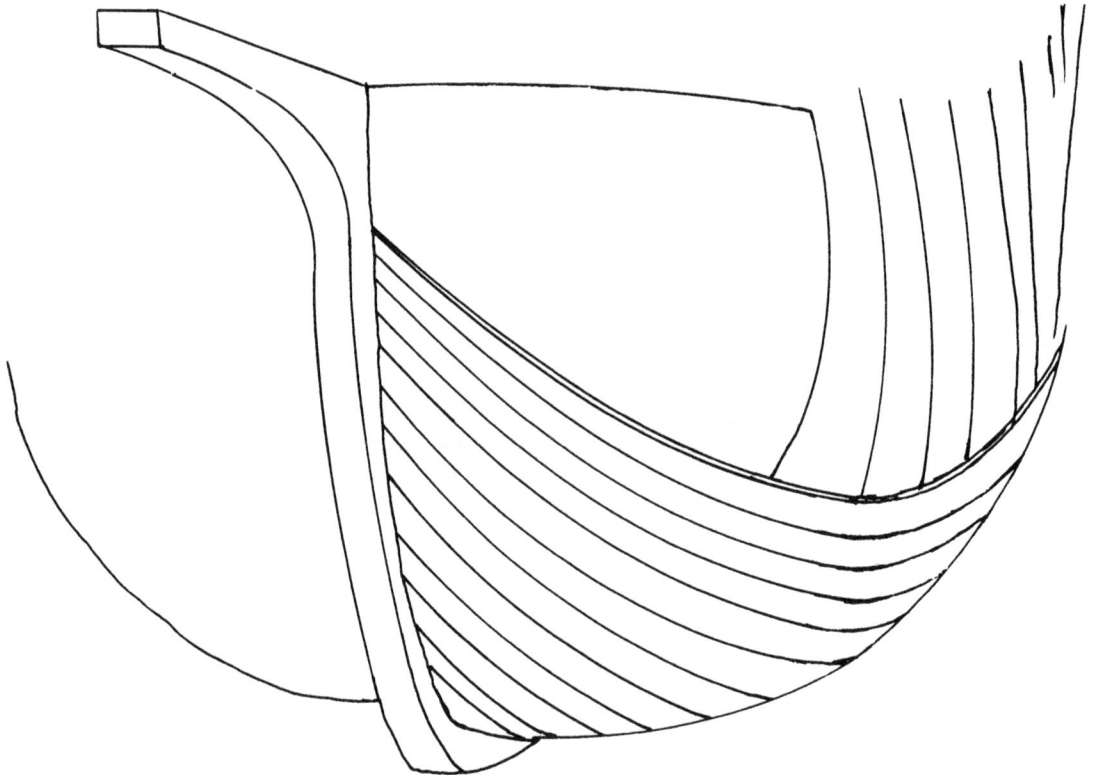

Fig. 3-8. The correct position of the planks. Wood should be removed from one side of the planks only to arrive at this form.

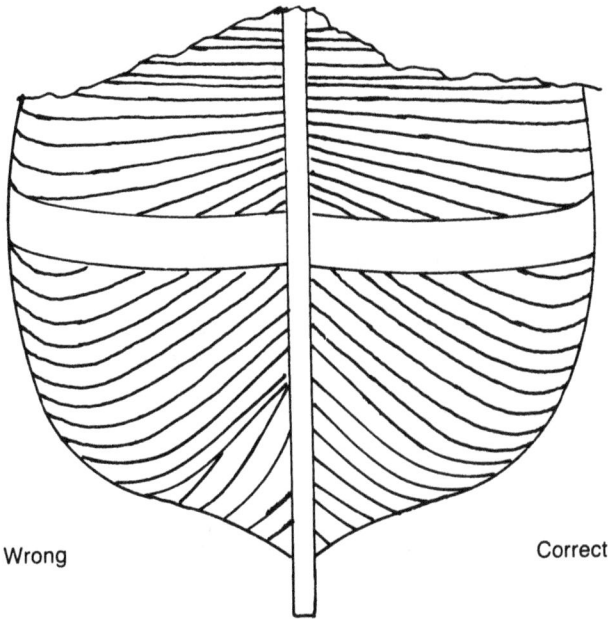

Wrong   Correct

Fig. 3-9. (left) Planking the correct and the incorrect ways are shown here. The upper portion of the planking also indicates the symmetry you should have on your planking on both sides of your hull.

Fig. 3-10. (above) A very small gap can exist between your planks. You can remove this gap if you sand the inside edge of the plank just a small bit before you install it.

previously drawn on the planks. If you use this method be careful that the two planks remain in the same relationship one to the other and that the cuts or the sanding is done evenly. You can also perform this operation with a jigsaw but I prefer the sanding method.

Dick Roos likes to use a finger plane to do the same thing, since he works inside his house and does not like to raise too much sawdust if at all possible. I am sure there are other methods to reach the same result of having the plank shaped to the desired form.

This same process will be used later in the second planking, or the first planking if you are using just single planking. If the model is single planked and of the kit variety, make sure you have enough frames to adequately plank the model smoothly. If in doubt, try to obtain some other wood planks and make the model a double-planked model, but be sure to remove the appropriate thickness from the bulkhead's dimensions to compensate for the extra thickness of the planks you are adding. Most of the plank-on-bulkhead kit models have a thick first-planking material and a thin second-planking material.

The actual procedure in fixing planks for the first layer follows. After you have formed the plank to its proper shape, apply glue to the back side and the edge of the plank that will make contact with the frames and the other edge of the plank already in place. By glue I am referring to the aliphatic resin type wood glue.

Do not use too much glue in this operation since it will only make the job harder. Too much glue will not improve the joint at all. The best way is to smooth the glue on the back of the plank with your finger. Have a wet rag handy to wipe your finger off prior to laying the plank.

Place the forward end of the plank at the stem and alongside the existing plank above it. Use a clamp to hold the plank in position or make a *stem jig* to hold the end of the plank where you want it along with a clamp. This stem jig (FIG. 3-11) is a piece of wood cut to the curve of the stem where the planking meets the stem. With the end of the plank being held in place, bend the plank around to the bow area and hold it down. Insert a push-pin into the closest bulkhead to the stem up against the plank and drive it home so that the head of the pin will hold the plank firmly in place and up against the previous plank.

Proceed to the next bulkhead and do the same procedure. FIGURE 3-12 shows some of the push-pins in place along a typical hull.

Be sure to check the plank for its smoothness of run along the line of the last plank laid. If it does not follow the last plank between the bulkheads, use a clamp or a pair of locking forceps to hold the plank in place next to the previous plank. If things are done correctly, clamping will not be necessary, but it helps to make sure the run of the planking is smooth and even, with no bumps and hollows.

If an excess of glue comes out between the planks while you are planking, use the wet rag to clean it up before it dries. It is much easier at this stage to simply wipe the glue off before it dries than it is to have to sand it off after it has dried. Do not worry about the end of the plank that will extend beyond the end of your stern. You can cut it off once the plank has dried, then sand the plank to the contours of the stern.

After you glue a plank to the hull, place its twin plank on the other side of the hull in the same location. You can install a plank on the port side under the wale, then do the same on the starboard side, then go back to the port side and install a plank just above the garboard plank, then switch to the starboard side and install the fourth plank just above the garboard plank.

Having installed the fourth plank, prepare the next set of planks for installation. Prepare four more planks, two twin sets for the upper and lower portion of your hull, by contouring and sanding them to shape. Use the bow-bending jig if needed.

When all is ready, remove the push-pins. Before you proceed to install the next set of planks port and starboard, first make sure that the run along the plank just installed is smooth and clear of any obstruction.

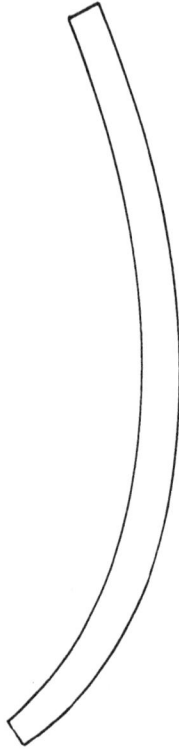

Fig. 3-11. A piece of wood cut to the shape of your bow curve at the stem. Clamp this piece of wood to the stem right at the outer edge of your rabbet to help hold the bow plank in place until the glue has had a chance to set.

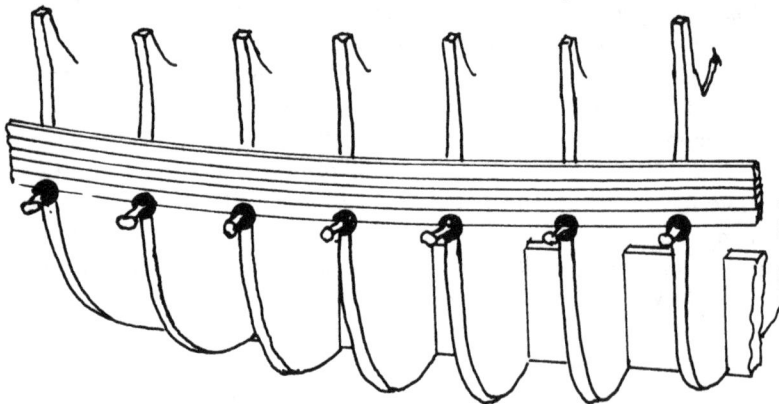

Fig. 3-12. Installing the planks one by one with the use of push-pins. This method of installing frames is useful for bulkhead-type construction only.

Sometimes, excess glue will collect around the push-pin, bulkhead, and plank just installed. You must file or cut away this glue with your knife, rasp, or file. Check by laying the next plank alongside the one just installed before you apply glue and install the next one.

Mark the location of your bulkheads as you plank. This will be a great help in construction when you install your second set of planks. Take care not to lose your waterline mark. Follow this same procedure, planking above and below until you meet in the middle.

To shape the last plank on both sides, obtain a piece of paper, lay it atop the planked area while covering the area not yet planked, and run your finger along the area not yet planked to give you an outline of the final plank required to finish the hull with your first layer. Since you have used your eye only in the first operation, you will find that despite your best efforts the last plank will not be the same on both sides as it should be. This is all right on the first layer of planking since it will be covered up and you do want to follow a different pattern of planking on your second layer of planking. It also demonstrates that you will need some help in laying out your planks for your second layer if the planks are to come out correctly, since doing it by eye will not work.

To obtain the best results, you can and should follow the same procedures used by the scratch builder when he planks his model. The only real difference is that the scratch builder will not fully plank his model since he wants the frames he spent so much time making to show on his final model, while the kit builder and the scratch builder who uses bulkheads must plank the entire model. FIGURE 3-13 shows one of Henry Bridenbecker's models, which leaves only part of the planking left out to show the frames. FIGURE 3-14 shows another one of Henry's models with the frames fully exposed. Some scratch builders opt to plank the entire model, even though they have built up the frames. Ed Marple's model of the *Sovereign of the Seas* is fully planked (FIG. 3-15).

FINAL LAYER OF PLANKING

So far I have discussed the shaping of the solid hull to prepare the ship model for planking, as well as the work required for the plank-on-bulkhead kit builder to prepare his model for the second and final layer of planking. The scratch builder who has prepared his frames or bulkheads is also now ready to plank his model. No matter which of the three types of ship models you are building, use the following procedure to obtain the best and most accurate result. If you have run into trouble with your first layer of planking on the plank-on-bulkhead type of kit, perhaps the following will help.

Some modelers use liquid glues to glue their planks into place. This procedure has its advantages: the glue dries very fast, and holds the plank almost instantly in place. The disadvantages, however, are that you do not have time to move the plank into position once you have placed it, and you do not know how long the bond will last.

The liquid glues are relatively new and might not last over the years. If you do use the "hot stuff" to cement your planks into position, you should also dowel them into the bulkheads using the aliphatic resin glue with the dowels, just to make sure they do not come adrift. This results in more time than the conventional way using the aliphatic resin glue in the first place, but if you are in no hurry and do not have a schedule to meet, this is of no importance.

Two other tools you need to do your doweling work to make the job of planking and doweling easier are a pair of diagonal flush cutters and a pair of end flush cutters. They are used to cut the ends of the dowels off after you have inserted them into the planking. The flush cutters will save you the large amount of sanding over you must do if you use the nonflush type of cutter, which leaves more of the wood sticking out. You can get by with just one pair, but one of each type of flush cutter will save you a lot of work.

Wale

Next, install the wale itself. It follows the proper line of the sheer of the vessel, and must be taken off of the plans. On a solid-hull or a plank-on-bulkhead model with the first layer of planking completed, draw the wale line onto the hull itself as a guide to install the wale. The scratch builder with a set of frames will of course have marked each frame where the wale will be located.

The wale is installed the same way as the first

Fig. 3-13. Henry Bridenbecker's scratch model of the Hannah, *a colonial schooner of 1775, showing one method of planking your model and leaving an open area to show the frames.*

Fig. 3-14. The Brig Irene, *another one of Henry Bridenbecker's fine models, shows the effect of using different wood colors to make the frames.*

layer of planks, except that you must take care that the end of the wale fits into the rabbet. As a general rule, the wale is a thicker plank than the rest of your planks (FIG. 3-1). Bevel the end of the wale if necessary to fit into the rabbet of the stem. Glue this end into the rabbet and the adjacent frame. Lay the wale around the bow and hold in position with clamps, wire twisted around a frame, or a push-pin (with solid-hull or single-planked bulkhead models).

Dowel the end of the wale into the stem and knighthead timber. The dowel should be parallel to the stem for maximum strength to make sure the wale at the stem is firmly held in position. If you are working on a framed model, next dowel the wale to each frame as you go from the stem to the stern of the ship.

Make sure that the wale fits into the stern structure of the ship when you reach this point. Since this timber holds the model ship together, it should be one piece of wood. You can make it out of more than one piece of wood if you want to follow real practice, but you must then scarf-join it so that it will act like one piece of wood. It is generally one piece of wood in most ship models due to the strength requirement. This is one area in which the modeler who is building his model with the bulkhead method can be a little fancier than one making a plank-on-frame model in that he can afford to scarf-join the wale without worrying about the loss of strength to the ship model.

The shape of the wale plank itself should be taken off at points along the hull and shaped before installation. Do not try to shape a plank after it has been installed on the ship. Mark the top of the wale line from the plans onto the ship. Next lay a piece of cardboard along the side of the ship from end to end, with it just touching the top of the wale line drawn on the ship at the midship frame. Let the cardboard lay on the hull naturally without forcing it. Using proportional dividers or a compass, mark the cardboard using the wale line on the hull as a guide. The bottom marks on the cardboard will indicate the shape of the bottom of your wale. Take the cardboard off the hull and lay it on the wood material you will make your wale out of.

Keeping the dividers the same width (the wale is the same width throughout), again locate the top of the wale onto your material, which is lying flat on your table. It is then an easy matter to again lay out the bottom of your wale to obtain the exact shape of the wale on a flat surface. Cut out this shape and place it on the hull. You will see that it fits right into place just as it should if everything was done as it should have been. The wale of Henry Bridenbecker's model (FIG. 3-16) and the multiple wale of Ed Marple's model of a larger warship (FIG. 3-17) are shown by the dark plank running above the hull planks.

Bilge Stringers

If you are building the framed ship model, the next hull plank to fix is the bilge stringers. (If you are a solid-hull or plank-on-bulkhead kit builder who has already installed one layer of planking on the hull, you do not have to worry about this part of the construction.) This adds the final strength timber to the ship model for the framed type and should be installed on the port and starboard side of the keel. You must follow the same rules of installation of planks as the bulkhead-type builder followed. That is, that

Fig. 3-15. Ed Marple's model of the Sovereign of the Seas *under construction, showing the planking in progress. Notice the use of two different types and colors of wood in the planking.* (Photo courtesy of Ed Marple.)

Fig. 3-16. The Hannah by Henry Bridenbecker, again showing the planking on the other side of the hull, which Henry fully planked. Notice the smooth run of the planking and the clean look of the dowels.

Fig. 3-17. The H.M.S. Royal Katherine is another excellent built model by Ed Marple showing the use of two different kinds of wood in the planking. The wales are also shown, along with his finished gunports. (Photo courtesy of Ed Marple.)

once you install a plank on the port side, you should install its mate on the starboard side before you add another plank on the port side. Alternate your planking.

On real ships, there was an inner set of planks as well as the outer set of planks. Most ship modelers do not go to the extent of installing the inner set of planks since it cannot be seen. A single set of bilge stringers will do for most models. Install them where the ceiling (floor) of the real ship is located. Dowel the planks into place inside the hull, just like the planks on the outside of the hull.

In the case of the bilge stringer, work out from the middle, instead of from one end. Start at the midship frame, drill a hole for the dowel, and then glue and dowel the plank. Next, drill and dowel the next frame forward of the midship frame, then the frame just aft of the midship frame. Go to the next one forward, then aft, etc.

This procedure will require the removal of the jig for the frames, but since your wales are already in place the alignment of your frames should not be affected. The model shown in FIG. 3-18 is a good example of what the inner beams should look like. In an open model such as this one, you must install all of the inner beams because they are all visible on the completed model.

Beam Shelf

The *beam shelf* is next. This plank is not required of the plank-on-bulkhead model builder because the top of the bulkheads will perform the same task as

Fig. 3-18. An excellent model of the Ship from Kalmar built by Henry Bridenbecker. It shows off to perfection the inside details of this type of ship.

the beam shelf and the deck beams of the plank-on-frame model. The beam shelf is the timber that supports the deck beams, which in turn support the deck. At this time, you can take the model out of the jig to do work on it because the frames are now rigidly supported by the wales and the bilge stringers.

The main item to make sure of when installing the beam shelf is that it is in the proper location along the entire length of the hull. This is one of the important areas where the waterline that you drew on your frames comes in very handy. Carefully measure from the waterline to the top of your beam shelf from the plans and mark the location for each frame. It does not hurt to check the measurements on both port and starboard frames to make sure they are the same, as they should be. Take great care with this step because the height of your deck at the side of the ship is determined by the positioning of the beam shelf.

Once you have located and marked this line, position the beam shelf in place and hold it there with some clamps while you check to see how much wood must be beveled off the surface of the beam shelf (FIG. 3-19). After you have completed the shaping of the beam shelf, install it in place and dowel it. Use clamps to hold it in place until it is dry, then dowel. When doweling, use the same procedure you used for the bilge stringers, starting at the midship frame. Be sure to observe the sheer of the deck (the curve from fore and aft) if there is one. You should have done so when you drew in the deck line from the plans using your waterline mark as the reference point.

FIGURE 3-20 shows Ed Marple's *Conqueror* ship model under construction, with the lower beam shelf in place. Notice that the gun ports are already cut to ensure that the deck will be in the proper place when the cannons are installed. If you have more than one deck on your model, you will have to install more than one beam shelf (FIG. 3-21).

Spaces between Cant Frames

The next step is to fill in the first few spaces between the cant frames at the bow area. You have already filled in the spaces between the stem and sternpost, as well as between the frames and the keel, being sure to blend it all in so that the planks will fit into the rabbet.

Fig. 3-19. A detail showing the removal of the excess wood from the beam shelf prior to installation of the deck beam.

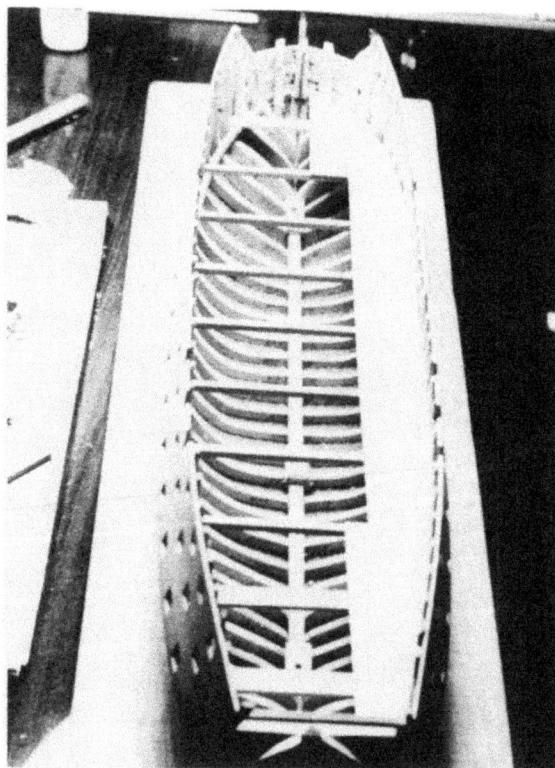

Fig. 3-20. The Conqueror by Ed Marple, here showing the internal construction and the beginning of the installation of the lower deck. Notice that the main deck beams are the only ones installed. This deck will be fully planked. (Photo courtesy of Ed Marple.)

Fig. 3-21. Another view of Ed Marple's Conqueror *showing to advantage the beam-shelf installations for both the lower and upper deck.* (Photo courtesy of Ed Marple.)

Fig. 3-22. H.M.S. Royal Katherine *by Ed Marple showing the blunt bow, which is one of the more difficult areas to plank.* (Photo courtesy of Ed Marple.)

The filler between the cant frames at the bow area was done in the real ship construction, and helps support the *hawse holes* if you have them on your model. The hawse holes are the holes in the bow area for the anchor rope to pass through (FIGS. 3-22 and 3-23).

You must also dowel the cant frames in place, and glue them. You might exert a lot of strength on the bow area when you plank, so the stronger it is the better.

Garboard Strake

The garboard strake is next (FIG. 3-24). This plank is one of the more difficult to install, but must be installed by all of the builders: solid, plank-on-bulkhead, and plank-on-frame. This is also one area in which the scratch builder has an advantage over the kit builder. The garboard strake is usually a little larger than any of the other planks, and it helps if

you have a larger plank you can use to cut out the shape of the garboard strake. If you are building a kit, you can use one of your planks, but I would suggest that you try to obtain at least one wider plank for this one plank.

This task is approached like many others. First make yourself a template of the plank. I used to have trouble figuring out just how high up the stem area this plank went. This question was resolved for me by Henry Bridenbecker. Take a piece of masking tape and fix it to the midship area, then press fit it into the rabbet of your model. Then pull it taut and let it run smooth to both the bow and the stern, letting it fall where it naturally will. Run your fingernail along the rabbet of the keel, stem, and sternpost area, and you will have a line of the bottom run of your garboard plank. Carefully lift this off your model and place it on your piece of wood. Cut or sand the unwanted part of the wood away.

Fig. 3-23. The Baltimore clipper ship Elizabeth, *which I built from a study by Howard Chapelle's books on these ships. Notice the easy run of the bow, which makes this type of ship much easier to plank.*

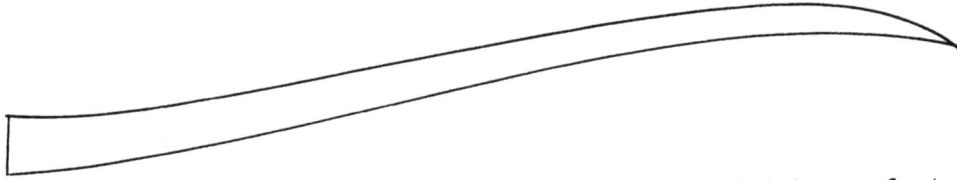

Fig. 3-24. A typical garboard strake laid out on a flat piece of paper.

it on your piece of wood. Cut or sand the unwanted part of the wood away.

You now will have a plank that will fit nicely into the rabbet from the sternpost, along the keel, and into the stem, and it will even be cut to exact length. Just for the fun of it, you can check to see how accurate your work is by comparing the garboard plank for the port and starboard sides of the hull. They should be mirror images of each other. There should not be any curve on this garboard strake because it would affect the rest of your planks. The top of the plank should be level and flat along the hull after it is installed to leave you with a level surface to work from when installing your next plank.

Battens

The final step before the actual planking should begin is to install your *battens* (FIG. 2-24). Battens are strips of wood you install at various locations along your hull to assist you in planking.

Start at the midship frame at the turn of the bilge and run the first batten along the hull, letting it fall where it will. Lightly tack it into position to keep it there using sewing pins. The battens themselves can be just $1/16$-inch-square wood with predrilled holes for the pins to be inserted into the frames lightly.

Once the first batten is installed, divide the hull between the batten and the wale, and install another batten in the same way. Then divide the space between the middle batten and the garboard plank and install another batten. Again divide these spaces in half and install four more battens. The more battens you install, the easier and more accurate your planking will come out.

Once all of the battens are installed on one side of the hull, take the model up in your hands and check it from all angles by looking down the sides of the model, etc. In this way, you can correct any of the

batten locations that you do not like or that do not look correct when compared to the lines of the ship. This review will determine the run of your planks and might also influence you in determining the number of planks you will have on your ship, as well as the width of the planks.

Once you have made sure your battens are in the right place, install the same number of battens in the same locations on the other side of your ship. You must take care that the battens are identical in location on both sides of the ship. FIGURE 2-37 shows the beginning of the installation of battens on Ed Marple's model of the *Sovereign of the Seas*. Notice the lines drawn on Ed's frames for his wale.

If you are building a solid-hull or plank-on-bulkhead model, which make up most of the ship model kits now on the market, you have a choice of either placing actual battens on the model or of drawing the battens onto the hull. My personal choice is to put the battens on the hull, check to make sure they are correct, trace the battens onto the hull, and then remove them. These battens are only a guide to assist you in your planking. They will not become a part of the hull; you will remove them as you plank.

The beautiful run of the ship's planking is striking if done correctly, but is distracting from the ship model if it is not correct. Again, if you are going to paint the hull, then you do not need to be too much concerned with this aspect, unless you plan to make the planking lines show.

Some of the common faults with the planking of a hull have already been mentioned and demonstrated in FIG. 3-9. You can take all of these faults into account if you follow the proper procedures when planking. It makes no difference if your model is scratch or kit, the result can be the same. I have seen some very fine models that were built from kits but appear to be scratch-built, even if viewed by an expert. FIGURE 3-25 is a close-up view of my model of the *Friesland*, which is built from the Mamoli kit as a base, but has much more detail added. The doweling of the planks is there, but is difficult to see in this photograph. Dick Roos' Mantua kit model of a Dutch gunboat is shown in FIG. 3-26. Ed Marple's scratch-built model of the brig *Leon* is pictured in FIG. 3-27. FIGURE 3-28 shows Henry Bridenbecker's beautiful scratch-built model of the brig *Irene*. The final example is Bob Saddoris' model of an Egyptian ship (FIG. 3-29). All the models are done correctly. You can obtain these results if you follow the right procedures when planking. As far as I am aware, there are no kits that give you the details on how to plank correctly. They simply tell you to plank your model.

Stealers

Stealers (FIGS. 3-30 and 3-31) are used in planking, and you must know what they are before you start to plank. You must make a decision at this time that affect the use of stealers: what will be the width of your planks?

There will be areas in the bow and stern that cannot be properly planked because the number of planks which must be there will not fit or the area to be planked is too large for the number of planks which are to fit into that area. Here we are coming up against some of the rules that govern planking. One of these rules is that when you camfer a plank to fit, you should not cut away more than one-half its maximum width. If your plank in the midship area has a maximum width of ¼ inch, then no plank on the entire ship should ever be less than ⅛ inch in width.

Many ship's hulls did not require any stealers, but when one or more are needed, it is most important to know how to shape and install them. Stealers are used in actual practice, but only when needed.

Determining Number of Planks Needed

Now that you know what stealers are, you must figure out the number of planks you will need to plank your hull. The best way to determine this is to use proportional dividers. I do not know of another tool that will save you so much time in building ship models as the proportional dividers. You can get the same results using paper and pencil, and measuring everything with great care, but errors will creep in no matter how careful you are. The best way to automatically correct for these errors is to use proportional dividers and planking battens.

When measuring the area to be planked, be sure to measure the length of the bulkhead or frame off

Fig. 3-25. A picture of my kit model of the Friesland *by Mamoli under construction.*

Fig. 3-26. A Mantua kit model of a Dutch gun boat by Dick Roos is a fine example of what can be done with a kit model. Notice the smooth run of the planking.

Fig. 3-27. Ed Marple's model of the brig Leon based on the plans by Underhill. Notice the excellent installation of the dowels. (Photo courtesy of Ed Marple.)

65

Fig. 3-28. Henry Bridenbecker's Irene *was built from plans and data contained in the book by E. W. Petrejus. Notice the stern deadwood and the two lower strakes.*

Fig. 3-29. *An outstanding model by Bob Saddoris of an Egyptian ship, constructed with scarf joints and held together with line.*

Fig. 3-30. Bob Graham's model of the topsail schooner Eagle *under construction. Notice the location of the stealer plank under the stern (at the first clamp).*

Fig. 3-31. Rolly Kalajian's White Wings II, *again showing the proper use of a stealer at the stern (under the first plank after the opening).*

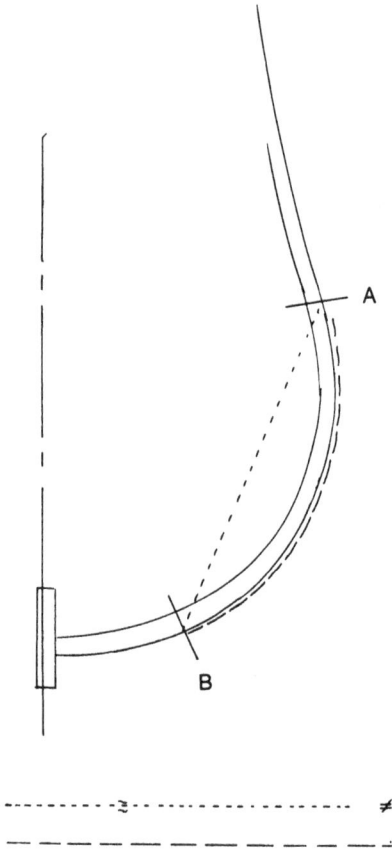

Fig. 3-32. *This drawing shows the different lengths you will obtain if you do not measure the hull properly. The distance from A to B is correct with the long dashed lines and incorrect with the short dashed lines.*

the hull with a piece of paper first, then lay it flat on a flat surface to make your measurements with the proportional dividers. The reason for this is shown in FIG. 3-32.

Also check the width of the planks with the kit model, even if the planks are already supplied. Many times the material supplied in the kits is too wide. This leaves the kit modeler with a decision to make. Do you go along with the kit, or do you get some more wood to complete the model? Remember, most kits have just enough wood to plank the model.

If you intend to plank the model to scale, you must obtain more wood. You can go this one step further and get a new supply of material to do the planking, but then you have invested even more money

in the kit. I have found that you can buy some additional wood to make up for that which is wasted when you cut the plank to the proper size, and that your extra effort is well worth it in the long run.

By all means do not be afraid to go beyond the kit, as long as you have made sure that you are still in the realm of reality in relation to the ship you are building. This is one area in which it really helps to be a member of a ship modeling club, like the Ship Modelers Association of Fullerton. All of the modelers I have had the good fortune to know have been only too happy to help a fellow modeler and assist him in any way they can. I think this is true of almost all ship modelers.

More Rules of Planking

You will need to know some more rules of planking before you can proceed. The real interest of the modeler concerns the length of the plank, the width of the plank, the number of dowels to install at what location, and the method to use to run the butts or ends of the planks on the hull (if you are going to follow the actual practice).

With kits, the planks supplied are all one length and go from the bow to the stern. This is not the way it was done in real ship construction. A board of 120 feet in length would be extremely difficult to handle even if a timber of that size could be found. This is the size of timber you are installing on your model to scale if you go from bow to stern.

Some of the better plans of ship models have the length of the planks shown so that there is no question as to their length. Usually, however, you must decide how long your plank is going to be. FIGURE 3-33 shows the general rule used for spacing the butts or joints of the planks along the hull of a ship. You can use this rule to determine the best length for your planks by working it out to your scale and drawing yourself a picture of what the plank butt or end spacing will look like. You will want to pay particular attention to the requirement of maintaining three planks between any butt joint on the same frame.

This is one of the reasons I mentioned earlier for marking the locations of your bulkheads when you were installing your first set of planks on your kit model. You can now draw these lines on your planks all the way down to represent the frames. You can also draw additional lines. These lines will give you clean, accurate locations for your dowels and will appear from the outside of the second planking as if you had framed the entire model. Also, the dowels in the second planking will go into all of your bulkheads, thus adding strength to the planks and the model.

You can follow the same procedure when you plank a solid-hull model. Measure your frame spacing and mark or draw the lines for your frames onto the hull. These lines are used for the location points of your dowels and the butt ends of your planks.

There is really no reason why you should not use short lengths of planks to do your planking, especially with a solid hull. It is really much easier to work with a short piece of wood than with a piece of wood that will go the entire length of the ship's hull. The plank is much easier to make since it is not so long, and you are less likely to make a mistake in measurement.

One thing I will add here is a tip from Bob Saddoris, another fine ship modeler who belongs to the S.M.A. According to Bob, if you want to make scarf joints in your planks, the only way to do it is the way it was really done. The procedure for this is just the opposite of what I just outlined. You lay out your entire plank first, putting the scarf into it on your bench, then install your plank with the scarf already in place. One of Bob's models with this type of scarf construction is shown in FIG. 3-29.

Dowels

One bit of work that is best done before you start planking is to make yourself a batch of dowels. You can make them out of any good hardwood, but bamboo is the preferred material for many modelers. I have made dowels out of bamboo, but also out of boxwood, walnut, and basswood, which all work quite well.

The procedure shown in FIG. 3-34 uses a drawplate to make the wooden dowels. Draw the wooden material through the largest hole, then work it down to the size of dowel that you wish to make by progressively going to smaller holes. I have found that it is easier to make these dowels in small lengths, rather than try to make one long dowel. The dowels themselves are very strong despite their fragile look.

After you have made a large batch of dowels,

a point on the end of the wood material prior to drawing it through the drawplate makes the dowel much easier to make.

You can either buy or make the drawplate itself. The price of one of these drawplates is rather expensive, so most modelers opt to make their own. It is an easy thing to do. Take an old piece of hacksaw blade and drill holes through it with your drill, starting at drill number 60 and working your way down to drill size 80. You might want to make a few larger holes than the drill size 60, but the wood stock you are making your dowels out of should be cut to small size to begin with. Do not clean the rough edges of the drilled piece of steel since they are what you will use to make your dowel. When you pull your material through the drawplate you have made, pull it through beginning at the rough edge, not the smooth side. In other words, pull your material through in the opposite direction from the way you drilled the steel.

I have made a pile of dowels in an hour or two with very little effort. Like everything else, once you get the hang of it, it is easy. If you do not care to make your own dowels, you can purchase them from several sources.

If you do not want to dowel the planks on the model ship you are constructing, then there is no real reason for you to butt-plank the hull either. Go ahead and use the full plank the entire length of your ship, although I think it is more difficult to do. I think that an error of omission, although you should avoid it if possible, is all right on a ship model if you have strong reasons for it. The real thing to watch out for is the error of putting something on your model that does not really belong there. Always check the plans or do further research into your model before you add something to it.

The number and location of the dowels is also of importance, assuming you are going to dowel your model. It is really a very small addition to your model to dowel, only takes a little more time, and adds very much to the overall appearance of your work, not to mention the added strength it gives. A rule to follow in the installation of dowels is that if the plank is less than 8 inches wide, only one dowel should be used. If the plank is more than 8 inches but less than 11 inches wide, then alternate between single-dowel and

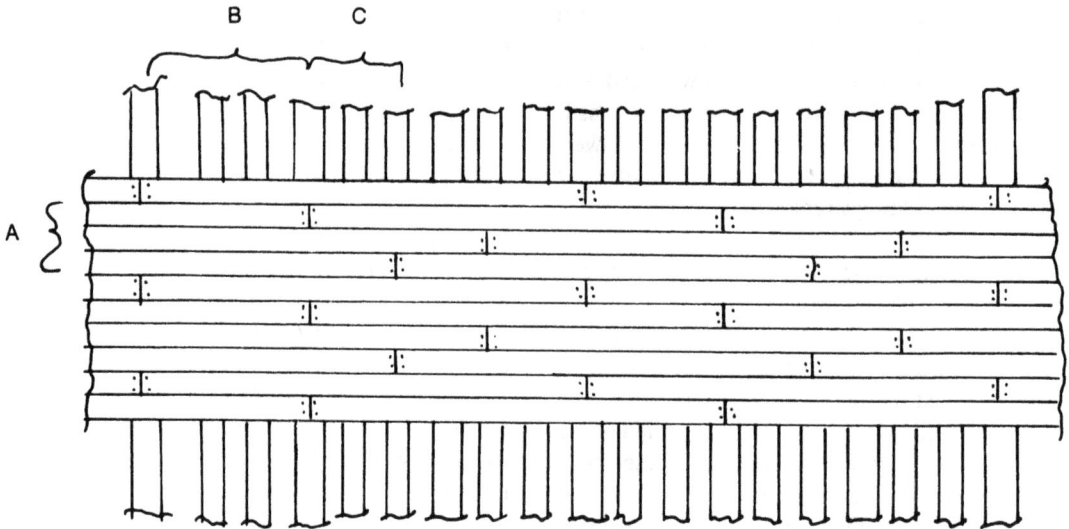

Fig. 3-33. An example of how your doweling and the location of your butts or the ends of your planks are supposed to be. A states that there must be three planks between any two butts on the same frame. B states that there must be 5 feet between two butts on adjacent planks. C shows that there must be 4 feet between butts with a plank in between. It helps quite a bit if you draw this out on a piece of paper first before installing the dowels on your model.

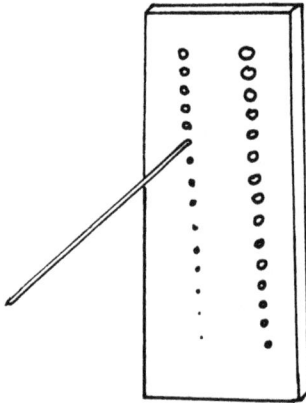

Fig. 3-34. A sample of a dowel being drawn through a drawplate to make the right size dowel. Bamboo is the usual wooden material used.

double-dowel installation at each frame. If the plank is larger than 11 inches, then use double doweling throughout. This rule is given in full scale, and you must take into account the scale in which you are working.

When doweling, first drill the hole into the location for your dowel. The hole should be one drill size bigger than the actual dowel. Then dip the dowel into diluted white glue and insert it into the hole. The swelling of the wood dowel will completely fill the hole, so you must make some allowance for the glue. Once you have installed the dowels and they have dried, you can cut off the ends of the dowels that are sticking out of the hull and sand them smooth with the hull.

Correct Run of Planks

Even if you do not butt-plank, you should at least try to obtain the correct run of the planks. The best method I have found to do this is explained in the next few pages. You should use it with all models, be they kit or scratch, when you plank a model.

The length of your planks should not exceed about 3 inches on a ⅛-inch-scale model, or about 6 inches on a ¼-inch-scale model. Many of the plank-on-bulkhead ship model kits are done to the scale of 1:75, which means your planks should not be longer than about 4½ inches.

After you have determined this dimension, you can lay out the butt positions of your planks before

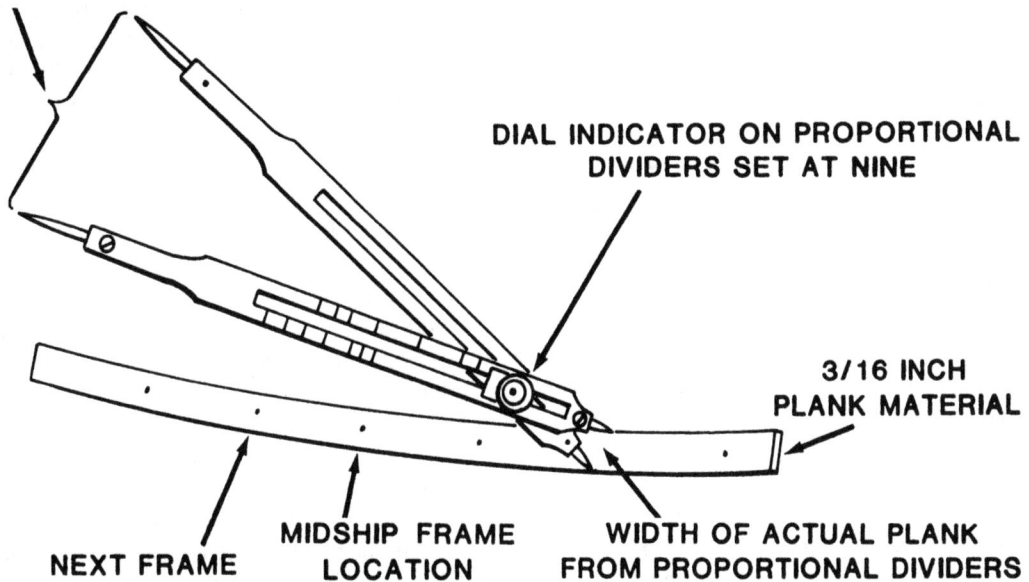

DISTANCE MEASURED BETWEEN
BATTEN AND WALE

DIAL INDICATOR ON PROPORTIONAL
DIVIDERS SET AT NINE

3/16 INCH
PLANK MATERIAL

NEXT FRAME

MIDSHIP FRAME
LOCATION

WIDTH OF ACTUAL PLANK
FROM PROPORTIONAL DIVIDERS

Fig. 3-35. The proportional dividers in use. (Drawing courtesy of Frederic Monfils.)

you even begin to plank. You should also consider the thickness of your planks because all of the planks are not the same thickness from the wale down to the garboard strake. If the thickness information is not shown in your plans, do not worry about it, with the exception of the obvious wale thickness. It is just another added detail for the meticulous scratch builder to be aware of and provide for if he has the information. Most of the plans of the much earlier ships of the fifteenth, sixteenth, and seventeenth centuries do not provide this type of information. An exception is the Swedish ship *Wasa,* in which case you have the real thing to work from.

You now start to measure the distance between your wale and your first batten. You will do this at the midship frame. Do not measure directly off of the frame, but put a piece of paper or tape on the frame, mark it between the wale and the first batten, take it off of the frame, and lay it on a flat surface and then measure the distance. Next, determine the width of your planks and the number you will use to fill in this space.

Planks will be a maximum of about 12 inches wide, which translates into a plank about 3/16 inch wide in 1:75 scale. If the measured distance between the wale and the first batten is about 1 11/16 inches, then you would have nine 3/16-inch planks to install to fill this space. It has never come out this even for me and you probably will need to shave off some of your plank material on each plank. Usually the space between the wale and the first batten will be less than the 1 11/16 inches needed, more likely something like 1 5/8 inches. This means that each of your planks will be slightly less than 3/16 inch wide at the midship frame.

This is where the proportional dividers come in. You have made your choice as to how many planks you desire to have on the midship frame between the batten and wale. Set the proportional dividers at the "nine" position on the dividers. Again make a paper or tape measurement from the wale to the first batten at the next frame over from the midship frame. Lay the paper flat on your board and measure the distance. Flip over the proportional dividers and you have the width of your board at this point. Mark this width on your plank and go to the next frame. FIGURE 3-35 shows this procedure. Do not be tempted to simply take the measurement off the frame directly, because error will creep in since the proportional dividers will no longer be measuring a flat surface but a curved one.

You can do the same procedure without proportional dividers, but it will take longer. Make a paper template of each frame space between the batten and the wale and mark it off into nine equal spaces using the triangle method of draftsmanship. This is more draftsmanship than I care to do, and I do not think it is as accurate as the proportional dividers because there is more chance of human error. Even the thickness of a pencil line can throw you off when it is multiplied many times over. With a large ship model, there might be a large number of planks, and each time you install one you might be adding to your error unless you correct for it.

With the proportional dividers, this error is automatically corrected in that you change the number of planks from nine to eight once you have installed your first plank, and proceed to measure once more between the newly installed plank and the first batten. Having only eight planks to go, you are now measuring a new space for eight planks with the proportional dividers, thus taking into account any error you might have unintentionally put into the first plank you installed, no matter how small. When you have completed your second plank, you will change the dial to seven planks and do the same thing. In this way you will fill up the area to the first batten with nine planks, all of equal dimensions and all going from the stem to the stern.

Again, if you come to a point where you must cut more than one-half of a plank's width, then you must install a stealer. You must also use a stealer if you must cover an area larger than the maximum width of your plank.

Once this first layer of planking is installed, then proceed to the lower area of the hull and plank the area between the garboard strake and the first batten above it. FIGURE 3-4 shows this procedure in progress on the hull of Ed Marple's model of the *Conqueror*.

Laying Butt Joints

While carrying out this procedure, you must also decide how you will lay out your butt joints. The rules stated for plank installation of butt joints (FIG. 3-33) are the minimum number of butt joints that you may have with the minimum number of planks in between the butt joints on one frame, and the minimum number of frames between each butt joint on the same plank.

One of the rules used in planking indicates that three planks must be between any butt joint on one frame, but you can have more than three planks. Given the maximum plank length, which in our example was 4½ inches long, and given that you will have so many planks between each batten, you can lay your planks out on a piece of paper and figure out just where your butt joints will be, since you also know where your frames are. Be sure that the butt joint does come at the same point as your frame. Also, take into account the sheer of the hull when you measure the length of your stock. It is no fun to measure and cut a plank only to find that it is a fraction too short.

The best way to avoid this shortage problem is to cut the plank a little long and test it at the location it is to be installed without gluing. In this way, you can correct any problems with its location and fit before you apply glue and fix the plank to the hull.

This procedure should be the method of operation for all aspects of the ship's construction. You do not want to ruin hours of work because you were in a hurry to install one small part of the model. One thing you must avoid in ship model construction is speed. The fun is making the model and figuring out how you are going to solve the multitude of problems that will develop in the ship construction process, not seeing how fast you can get the job done.

Determining Plank Length

You might decide that you do not want to install the planks in this way, but simply want to run the planks the full length of the hull as is provided in the kit. I am not advocating that there is only one way to build these ship models. I am simply trying to give you a choice. I have seen many fine and exceptional models without butt planking and without dowels in the hull. Some modelers do not like the "look" of dowels in the planking of the hull.

If you do want to follow the actual construction methods used by the builders of the real ships, then you will want to install the dowels and also incorporate the butt system into your planking. The butt system also helps you determine the lengths of the planks you will need when planking your model. I have chosen as my example planks of a maximum length of 4½ inches long. This maximum length might be a little longer than this or a little shorter, as determined by measurement against the hull before you begin to plank the model.

On a piece of paper, draw out the length of one run of the planks from stem to sternpost. Either count the number of frames or the number of lines you have drawn on your hull to represent the frames, or simply mark off the 4½-inch marks. Check to see how long the last plank will be. Say the planks come out to be three pieces of plank at 4½ inches and the last plank is 4 inches long. Then you can use this length on this layer of planks. Further drawing on the next several layers of planks might result in a plank of less than ½ inch. This plank will be too short. Do not install a very short plank that will only cover two or three frames because this was generally not done. Either slightly extend the length of your planks to make them a little longer than 4½ inches or a little shorter to avoid this short plank.

This is one reason why you should draw out the first layer of planks between the wale and the first batten before you begin to lay the planks. It might sound like a lot of extra work, but it really is just fun, and it really does not take very long. The time you will save will be more than you will lose later if you have made a mistake in laying out the butt joints of your planks. It is the same as a person who wants to sew a pattern on a piece of material and does so without going through the process of measuring, only to find that the pattern does not match when he goes to sew it together. The hull of a ship model should show the same pattern throughout the run of the planking, as was done on the real ship.

Using a Pencil

One important item to mention while on the subject of planking is the critical requirement for a very sharp pencil. This pencil, which is used for all the measurements for your planks must be sharp and able to make very fine lines. The use of a dull pencil will lead you to make mistakes in forming the planks.

You will not know exactly how much wood to take off because of the thickness of the line you are using as a guide. The thickness of a pencil line might not seem like much to you, but when it is multiplied by the number of planks, a very large error can result which will ruin your entire effort. The pencil I use is a number 6H hard lead pencil, which will draw a very fine line.

PLANKING

If you don't have a set of proportional dividers, you can do the planking with the 6H pencil. The fine 6H pencil should be used with or without proportional dividers, but it becomes even more essential without them.

First Layer of Planks below the Wale

Having decided on a length for your plank, take the first plank, which is cut a little long, and place it at the stem. Bend it around the bow area to lay where it will be installed. If the plank does not fit into the stem correctly, remove it and cut the plank to fit the angle. Again place it at the stem and fit it around the bow area. If it lies properly, fine. If not, again remove it after marking the underside of the plank with the sharp 6H pencil where it does not fit and cut or sand to shape. Test-fit it again, making sure it makes proper contact with all the frames and the wale or plank upon which it lies.

Once you are satisfied that the plank will fit properly, set the end of the plank into the rabbet of the stem and hold it there with a clip and a piece of wood (FIG. 3-36). Bend the piece of wood (which must already be bent into shape) around the bow and hold it in position with another clamp. With the sharp 6H pencil, mark the center of each frame on the piece of wood from the first cant frame at the bow to the last frame where your butt will be. The last mark on the plank indicates where you will cut it. This location should be at the middle of the frame because the next plank, which will abut the plank you are now installing, also must have a firm landing on the same frame.

These marks you are putting on the plank have a dual purpose. They not only indicate where the dowel

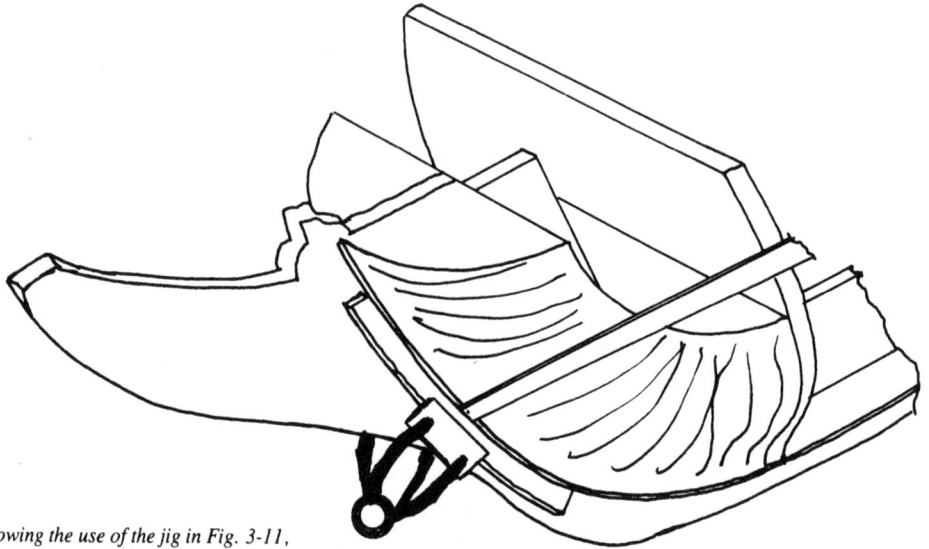

Fig. 3-36. A drawing showing the use of the jig in Fig. 3-11,
along with a clamp to hold it in place while installing your
bow planks.

locations will be, but also are used to determine the
length of the plank at this point. Using a piece of paper, you have already measured the length between
the wale and the first batten and have determined the
number of planks you will install to fill this area. Instead
of using the proportional dividers, mark each frame
with the determined distance required to obtain the
number of planks in that space. Next, take this distance
at each frame and transfer it to the plank you have
just marked out. Say the distance measured on cant
frame number one is ⅛-inch. Transfer this distance
to the plank by measuring ⅛ inch down from the top
of the plank on the line just drawn to represent the
first cant frame. Going to the second cant frame, again
measure the distance off the frame. This might be
slightly larger than ⅛ inch. Transfer this slightly larger
distance to the second line drawn on your plank and
put a small point at this location. In this way, proceed
to mark the plank until you have located the width
of the plank at all of the frames. Then draw a line
to connect all of these points you have marked on
the plank, and cut off the excess wood to this line.
Again place the plank at the location it is to be installed. You should now see that the plank at its lower
edge makes contact with the little points you put on
your frames marking the width of your plank.

You can now use this plank as a template to cut

the plank to be used on the other side of the hull. Again,
with a sharp 6H pencil trace the plank and cut it out
to shape. Hold the two finished planks together. They
should match each other. The "new" plank just cut
out should install in the "old" plank's location and
look identical.

The completed plank should look something like
the plank drawn in FIG. 3-37. FIGURE 3-38 gives you
an example of how extreme some of these planks can
be and why careful measurement is a requirement if
you are to succeed in your planking effort.

You can now see the advantage the proportional
divider procedure has over the procedure just described.

After you have cut the plank to shape, install it
using a little bit of glue, as described previously. Use
clamps instead of push pins to hold the plank in position
since you do not want to destroy your frames. The
type of clamps used to hold the planks in position while
they dry are many and varied. Large and small paper clamps, clothespins, wire springs, and simply
pieces of wire twisted around the plank and the frame
have been used with great success. You can even resort to the method of holding the plank in place until
it dries. Another way is to use the instant glues, although I prefer the white glue for planking.

You next dowel the plank, starting at the end of

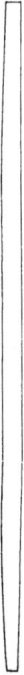

Fig. 3-37. A typical plank that has been shaped and is ready to install. If you are using the butt method (which is the correct way to install your planks or strakes), then this plank will be shorter, but still must be shaped.

the plank and working forward to the stem. Remove the clamp, wire, or other device holding the plank in place. Drill through the plank and frame with a pin-vise drill or other miniature drill, as described earlier. Dip the dowel in diluted glue and insert into the drilled hole, leaving a portion of the dowel sticking out at both ends to be cut off and sanded later. Proceed to dowel the entire plank. The number of dowels at each frame is determined by the width of the plank, as described earlier.

The last dowel installed is the dowel driven into the stem, and you must drive it parallel to the stem into the wood next to the stem, through the plank and not at a right angle to the plank. This method will give this critical area the strongest hold.

I do not believe that doweling is absolutely necessary for the strength of the hull. I have built a number of models without dowels and using white glue only. There is no doubt that dowels do strengthen the hull construction, and if installed they are just added insurance that your model will not come apart several years after you have built it. I have seen some models come apart in this fashion that were not doweled, but there might have been more problems than just the lack of dowels.

The last plank you will install will go into the sternpost. Fit this plank into the sternpost first, much like you fit the first plank into the stem. Then run the plank back to the beginning of the last plank you laid and carefully cut it to fill in the remaining space to complete your first layer or row of planking. I am assuming that you are duplicating everything you are doing on the other side of the hull as you go to avoid the possibility of warping your hull.

When you go under the counter at the aft end of the ship, you will need to bevel the planks to match the curve of the counter. If you follow the practice of checking your plank on the hull to make sure it fits properly, then you will have no problem. You can also bevel the other side of the plank so that it is parallel to the edge of the frame on which it will be fixed. This method will save you problems with the next plank to be laid.

You can now see the advantages to laying the planks with the butt method instead of laying them in one long piece, as is recommended by the kit manufacturers. It seems like it is more work, but actually it is easier. Trying to lay the entire plank on the frame and getting all of the bevels right, as well as fitting the plank into the stem rabbet and the sternpost rabbet would be a difficult thing to do correctly with any high degree of accuracy. This is one reason why all kits I have built so far make no mention of the rabbet.

Cutting the rabbet into the stem, keel, and sternpost unit with an X-ACTO knife or other tool does take some time and must be done carefully, but the result is well worth the effort. Another way of doing the rabbet is to add an additional layer of wood to the outside of the stem, keel, and sternpost, but this will also require taking off the unit thickness of this additional wood from the stem, keel, and sternpost, and might be more difficult than just cutting the rabbet into the skeleton assembly as required.

Most of the kit models have a ridge along the rabbet line of the model, which is a result of not having a rabbet. For the craftsman the use of the rabbet and the individual plank-butt method is the only way to go, and can be done on kit models as well as scratch-built models if you so desire.

Area between the Wale and First Batten

You will now have successfully installed your first layer of planks below the wale on both sides of the ship. Continue to fit the rest of the planks in the same fashion until you have filled up the space between the wale and the first batten on both sides of the ship. Next, remove the first batten and proceed to plank between the already installed planks and the second batten. Be sure to take into account that you did not install the last plank of the first batten area. You must adjust the proportional dividers to include this plank. This means that if there are nine planks in your second area between the first and second batten, the you should set your proportional dividers for ten planks to include the one plank you have not yet installed. This method also helps you make sure that any errors you have made will be compensated for by the proportional dividers.

Keel Area

Before completing this area of planking, you should shift your attention to the keel area. You have already installed the garboard strake on both sides of the hull. You should now install the planks between the garboard plank and the first batten above this plank. Proceed in the same way you did for the area below the wale. You will now be planking from the wale down and from the garboard strake up. The

Fig. 3-38. An example of a very difficult planking job done by Henry Bridenbecker on his model of the ship from Yassi Ada. Henry had to use two framing jigs to make this model due to the very high bow and stern.

reasons for this are the same as those stated earlier for the planking of kit models. It is much easier to plank in the midship area around the turn of the bilge than anywhere else on the ship, so it is also the best place to install your last plank.

In order to be able to go to the lower area and plank, it is essential that you have worked out your run of the butts of the planks, particularly if you are going to plank the entire hull. FIGURES 3-3 and FIG. 3-4 show this method of planking in operation by Ed Marple in his construction of the *Conqueror*. Ed is using lines drawn on his frames as battens after having already installed, marked, and removed the battens prior to beginning planking.

You can add to the planking of your ship's hull by using two different woods to plank with—one color for the upper portion of your hull and another for the lower portion. This can lead to some tricky wood joinery at the waterline, which is the line where you will wish to have the change of wood color. The waterline will not necessarily follow your sheer line, so be careful here. An example of this effect is shown in my completed scratch model of the clipper ship *Elizabeth,* named after my wife. FIGURE 3-39 shows this model, which was based on plans and instructions from Howard Chapelle's book *The Search For Speed Under Sail* and his book *The Baltimore Clipper*. FIGURE 3-15 also shows the use of two woods on Ed Marple's construction of his model of the *Sovereign of the Seas*.

When planking, do not forget to have a wet rag to wipe away any excess white glue that might squeeze out between the frames and planks, particularly at the stem rabbet area and the edges of

Fig. 3-39. An overall view of my scratch model of the Baltimore clipper Elizabeth *based on Chapelle's books.*

the planks which make contact with the frames. If you are doing a kit, then be sure the edge of the plank along the entire hull is clean of any glue buildup. It becomes very difficult to lay your next plank if there is glue in the way. Failure to remove this glue will leave large gaps between your planks, which must be avoided. If you have missed an area where glue has collected, then remove it with a knife, file it, then sand it smooth before you lay the next plank alongside it. You will avoid any abnormality in your process as you go if you follow this procedure, and continue to test-fit your next plank to the last one prior to fixing it with glue.

Second Layer of Planking

If you are following this planking method on a kit ship that you have already planked once, it is essential that you have carefully drawn in your frames onto the already planked first layer as a guide to doing your second layer of planking. The run of the butts of your second layer of planks, as well as the run of your doweling, will be determined by where and how accurately you have drawn your frames. The final hull will look well only if your frame positions were drawn accurately. It is well worth the added effort when you have planked your model correctly.

You should bend the bow area plank to shape before you glue it to the hull. Do not try to force-fit the plank to the hull because forcing will only add stresses to the finished ship model, which might lead to some of your planks pulling loose. I have seen this happen to some models that were not planked properly, so be warned that the best procedure to follow is to bend the plank on a form first, then install it. This is particularly true of the larger ships of the line and all ships with the blunt bow.

Using Stealers

If, during the installation of the planking, you run into an area where you must cut more than one-half from a plank's width or add more to its regular width to fill in the required area, then stealers will be required. If you determine the run of the planks carefully then stealers will not be required. I have not had to use stealers to plank any of my ships yet, but this does not mean that I will not someday run into a situation where I will have to use them.

You should use stealers only when necessary, and not to cover up bad planking methods. Like most other areas of ship modeling, if stealers are used correctly then they look correct and if they are used to try to cover up something then they look like they were used for that purpose. My main point is that you should plan for and use stealers if necessary to do the planking correctly and for no other reason. I do not believe that stealers were ever used in the upper areas of the planking where they could be seen, but were used mainly in the lower areas and below the counter where the natural sweep of the planks tended to open out fanlike at the stern, thus requiring stealers.

FIGURE 3-30 shows stealers and how they are checked into planks to continue the run. The stealer must start from the location of a frame. This is obvious to the scratch plank-on-frame builder, but not to the kit builder who has not drawn his frame lines in.

The proportional dividers will tell you at a glance if you will need to use stealers; the distance measured will be wider than the width of the planking material you are using. You will also be able to locate the ideal frame to begin your stealer. Increase your proportional dividers by one notch or plank to measure the distance at the sternpost. The model built by Dick Roos shown in FIG. 4-12 shows a stealer installation at the stern.

If you are building a kit model, one method of making your planking job look as if there was a rabbet installed is to plank the stem, keel, and sternpost after you have planked your model. This method is suggested in some kits, but care must be taken to make sure that the modified keel is not too thick. By planking the stem, keel, and sternpost, you make the garboard plank and the planks going into the stem and sternpost area smooth and flush with the planking, which is the way it should be. Again, test-fit the material to the edge of the plank first to make sure it is a good fit.

Number of Planks

If you are building a plank-on-frame model, decide how many planks you want to install on your ship. You can elect to leave a number of planks off the hull, thus exposing your frames and showing all of the work you have done. You also can install most of your planks and only leave a few of them off to show that you have indeed built up your frames. FIGURE 3-40 shows a fine example of Henry Bridenbecker's model, which is planked to show off the frames. Some scratch builders cannot leave off the planks even when they have built up the frames. Some examples are the models in FIGS. 3-41 through 3-44.

If you are building the model from a kit which is of the plank-on-bulkhead type or the wooden solid-hull type, then you must plank the entire hull to hide the portion underneath. FIGURE 3-45 shows a kit model that has been fully planked.

Final Plank

The final plank should be the easiest to install since it should be at the turn of the bilge in the middle of the hull. To install this plank, first fit the bow piece as described previously, then install the piece that fits into the stern area. This leaves you with the middle area to fill in.

The best way to fill in the middle area is to use masking tape to make a mold of the final plank to be fitted. Lay the masking tape along the opening in the hull, and run your fingernail along the edges to mark off the dimensions of your plank. Remove this tape and cut the final plank to this shape. The final plank should fit right into the open area snugly and cleanly, and will be glued and doweled into place. Just for the fun of it, you can also see if this same pattern will fit into the empty space on the other side of your model.

Fig. 3-40. Henry Bridenbecker's model of the ship from Yassi Ada showing the very high bow and stern areas.

Fig. 3-41. Bob Saddoris' model of the brig Leon, *again based on the book and plans by Harold A. Underhill. Notice that Bob chose to completely plank his model and hide the work he did on the frames.*

Fig. 3-42. An excellent example of an Egyptian ship built by Jack Elem. Again, Jack planked the entire hull.

Fig. 3-43. An excellent view of Jack Elem's Egyptian ship showing some of the deck detail. Notice how the inside of the hull planking must also be neat and clean since it can be seen.

Fig. 3-44. An example of a ship of the line by Ed Marple. This model is the H.M.S. Royal George. (Photo courtesy of Ed Marple.)

CLINKER-BUILT PLANKING

All of the planking described in this text so far has been *carvel-built planking*, or planking installed edge to edge, resulting in a smooth surface when the planking is completed (FIG. 3-46). There is another type of planking you will encounter in your ship modeling efforts, which is the *clinker-built* type of planking. This planking method overlaps each plank. FIGURE 3-47 shows the two different types of planking methods.

Clinker-built planking or simply clinker planking, was used by the Vikings when they built their ships. It was also used by the Dutch and the Swedish ship builders, one of the prime examples being the Swedish ship *Wasa*. FIGURE 3-48 shows the frame structure on the *Wasa*'s upper portion of the hull, with notches cut out in the frames to provide a firm landing for the clinker planks.

The general rule to follow with the clinker planks, which differs from the carvel type of planking, is that the overlap is twice the thickness of the plank. The garboard strake must be the first plank installed because the rest of the planks will overlap staring with this plank. There are other differences which have no relation to the carvel-built planking. The general rule is that the angle produced by any of the planks coming in contact with another cannot exceed the amount of bevel in relation to the width of the overlap. If the overlap is twice the thickness of the plank, the bevel cannot exceed this distance.

Fig. 3-45. My model of the Yacht Mary, *based on a kit by Mamoli. Some additions have been made, including doweling the hull.*

One other item which must be mentioned is that the clinker-built boat does become carvel-like, or smooth, when it enters the rabbet of the stem, keel, and sternpost. Bob Saddoris of the Ship Modelers Association of Fullerton has an excellent example of this type of construction (FIG. 5-9). All of the methods used will be explained in more detail when you come to the planking of ship's boats in Chapter 5.

OTHER CONSTRUCTION METHODS

Before going on to the next chapter, which will explain the construction of the deck beams and the planking of the deck—one of the most important aspects of your model to the average viewer—I would like to mention that there are other methods of ship model construction. One excellent example is one of Henry Bridenbecker's models of the ship from Kalmar which was used by the Hanseatic League in the thirteenth century (FIG. 3-49). He built this ship, using information obtained from Landstrom, Bass and Haws to draw his plans. This model was built over a mold because the frames were too big to bend properly. Henry made the mold out of good balsa wood and then laminated the frames with five layers, or thicknesses, of wood to arrive at the proper thickness of the frame. The hull was clinker-built, as was the real ship, and then removed from the mold. All of these molds must be heavily waxed to be sure that the ship itself will detach freely from the mold without sticking.

I will describe all of the methods I have used and also those methods I have seen used by other modelers in the Ship Modelers Association. I know that all of these methods have worked for a number of modelers. I also know that all of the modelers, myself included, have their own way of doing things, including the methods of planking. I am describing the methods I or other ship modelers have used successfully. You might find that you will need to modify some of the procedures to suit your own requirements for the model you are working on. I do not suggest that you must follow the procedures outlined in this book as

Fig. 3-46. My scratch model of the Elizabeth. I used a variety of woods on this model. Notice the outer hull planking of pear wood, and the inner bulkhead planking of red Honduras mahogany.

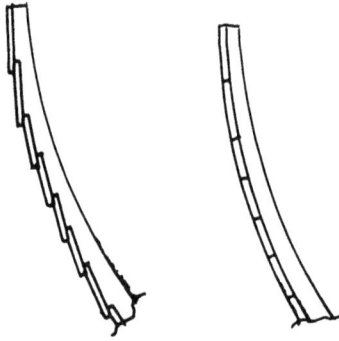

Fig. 3-47. The difference between clinker (left) and carvel (right) planking.

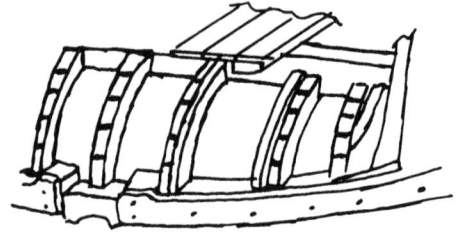

Fig. 3-48. A sketch of the upper bow areas of the Wasa, showing the location where clinker-type planks were installed and how the Swedish builders cut notches into the frames to accept the clinker planks.

Fig. 3-49. A final picture of the Ship from Kalmar by Henry Bridenbecker showing the beams that came through the planking. This is also an example of the clinker type of planking.

84

the only way of planking a model. The best advice I can give is to tell you to follow the actual construction procedures of the ship you are building as closely as possible to the way the real ship was built.

Read through the rest of the book before you begin to build your model. A few construction methods follow that you might wish to try before you begin the planking. I am following the procedure I used, but other modelers follow a different procedure. I planked my hull before I installed the deck beams, but Henry Bridenbecker likes to install his main wales, bilge stringers, and deck beam shelves before

he installs his planking.

In some kit models I have built, the deck planking is done on a false deck before the hull planking is even started. The reverse also can be done. So, read on before you make up your mind what order of things you will follow.

You should read and plan first before you begin to build. This is true of kit models, as well as the scratch models since much wasted time and effort can be saved this way. I have found that a complete study of a ship kit's plans might result in doing things in a different order than given in the kit model's instructions.

4

Planking The Deck

YOUR NEXT PROJECT IS TO BEGIN PLANKING YOUR deck and the *bulwarks,* or walls, of your ship. The *deck,* or floor, of the ship must have a structure on which it can be built, which consists of deck beams for a plank-on-frame ship, and in some cases for the plank-on-bulkhead type ship. Most kit models, either solid or plank-on-bulkhead, have false decks.

SOLID-HULL SHIP

In the case of the solid-hull ship, which can be both kit and scratch, the structure beneath the deck planks can be either the solid-hull wood itself, which has been prepared for the deck, or you can install actual deck beams. In the former case, you must carve out the solid hull and curve it to the shape of the deck. This curvature of the deck is shown in FIG. 4-1 and goes both port and starboard and fore and aft.

You will need to carefully shape the underside of the deck using the plans as your guide. You can remove the wood material with your knife, riffle files, sandpaper, a Dremel power tool, or any combination of these tools. You will need to be careful that you do not remove too much wood.

While you are removing the material, you must also decide if you want to hollow out the hull completely, which will be necessary if you install deck beams for your lower deck. For the last solid-hull model I built that was fully planked, I used the

that was fully planked, I used the deck-beam method to install the upper decks. I hollowed out the model to 1 inch or so below the deck-beam shelf of the lower gun deck, as shown in FIG. 4-2. I installed the deck-beam shelf, as for the plank-on-frame model. I then made the deck beams and fastened them in place.

In this particular model, I installed neon lights in the cabin area at the stern, the gun deck area in the forecastle, and the stern area below the captain's cabin. I mention this for two reasons. First, if you want to install lights in a ship of this period, use neon lights to avoid the problem of the light giving off heat, which might cause cracks in your ship model at a later time. The resistors that control the brightness of the neon light give off heat, so connect the resistors to the bottom of the ship's case with the wires going up through the pedestals into the ship's hull. Two more views of the pirate brig are shown in FIGS. 4-3 and 4-4. I have let the lights burn on this model for over 48 hours with no ill effects to the model.

Second, the neon lights give off a candlelike orange glow, which closely resembles the real thing. The lights on my pirate brig cannot be seen very well unless it is dark with all other lights turned off. This is as it should be, since very bright lights did not exist back in this time. The electrical schematic for the neon lights is depicted in FIG. 4-5.

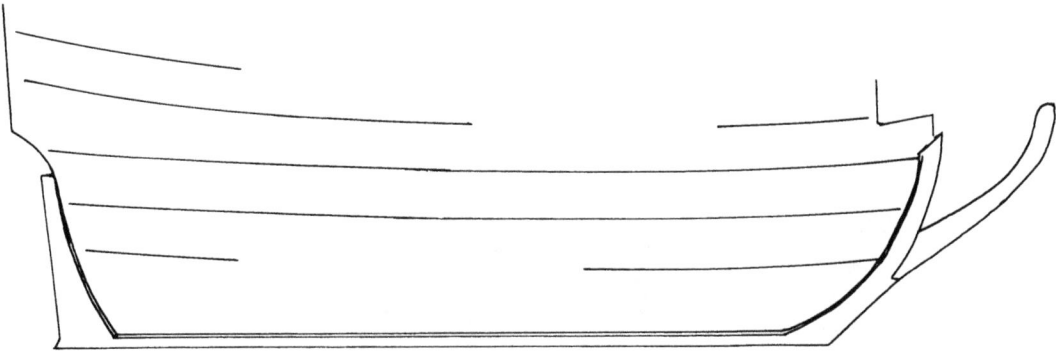

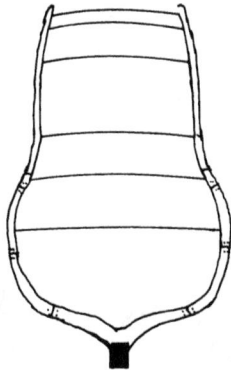

Fig. 4-1. An outline of a typical ship's hull, showing the run of the deck both fore and aft and port and starboard.

Fig. 4-2. My pirate brig which started out as a solid-hull kit by Bluejacket. I discarded most of the kit and planked the hull using basswood and ebony for the wales. I carved the stern section and quarter galleries from pear wood.

Fig. 4-3. A closeup shot of the pirate brig showing the hull planking of the solid hull.

Fig. 4-4. Another shot of the pirate brig. The head work was done with boxwood and the figure was carved out of a piece of ivory.

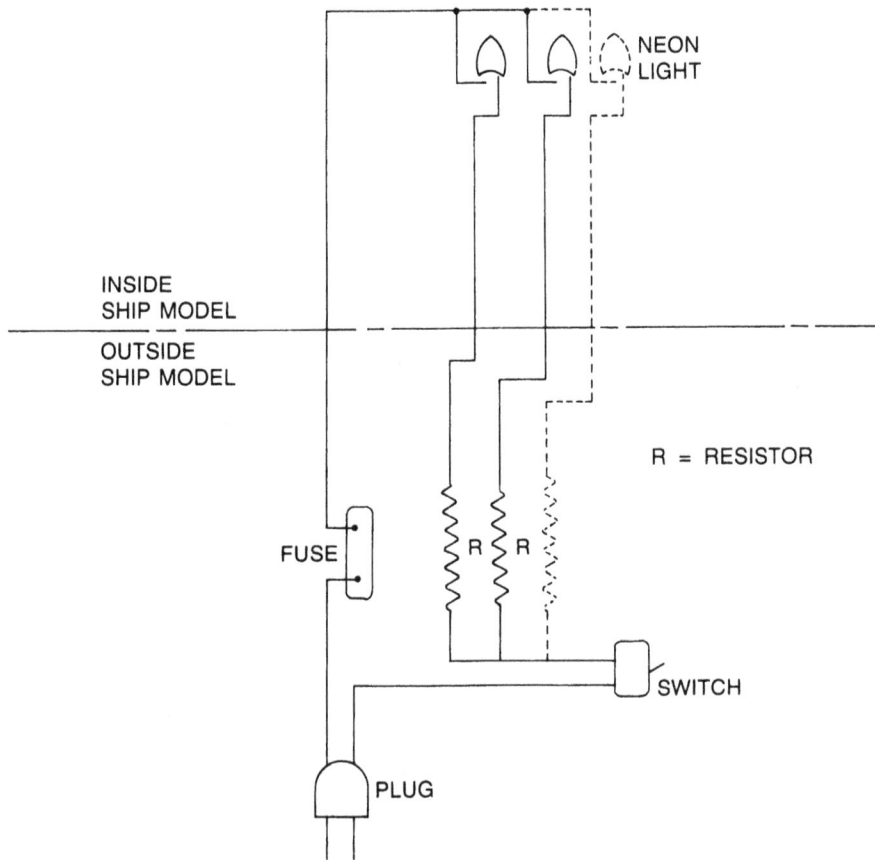

INSIDE
SHIP MODEL

OUTSIDE
SHIP MODEL

NEON
LIGHT

R = RESISTOR

FUSE

R   R

SWITCH

PLUG

Fig. 4-5. A schematic of the neon lights that are installed in the pirate brig. The lights have been installed and used since 1978 with no ill effects to the model.

Once you have cut out the inside of your solid hull to the proper depth for your deck and have installed your deck-beam shelves along the inside of the hull, as described in Chapter 3, you are ready to make your deck beams and install them onto the deck-beam shelves. I am assuming that you have carefully installed the deck-beam shelves with reference to your plans.

Before you install your deck-beam shelves and your deck beams, you should thin out your bulwarks or the "walls" of your ship to make the installation of the shelves easier. This is particularly true of the solid-hull kit models, since all of them come with the bulwarks much too thick, to avoid damage in shipment. The best tool to use is a sharp chisel to cut the wood. First draw a line along the top of the bulwark as a

guide, then cut down and out.

For the solid-hull model, it is best at this point to have a cradle in which you can support your model. The bulwarks at this point are rather fragile, and they should be carefully cut away as thinly as is possible, since you are going to install the inner bulwark planks on the inside of your hull.

When you are installing the beam shelf for your deck beams, be careful you do not run the dowels, if used, through your already installed outside planking. FIGURE 4-6 illustrates how to measure the depth of drill penetration into the wood prior to inserting the dowel to hold the beam shelf. If you have more than one deck level on your ship, you will need to install a beam shelf for this deck also.

The next step is for you to make your deck beams.

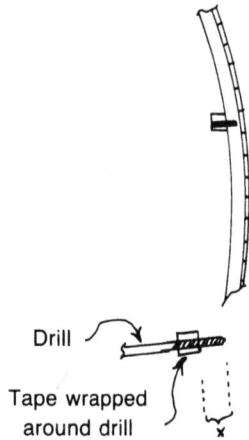

Drill

Tape wrapped
around drill

Fig. 4-6. A sketch showing one method of measuring the depth of your drill penetration into the wood by wrapping tape around your drill.

The method I have used and found very successful is to select a piece of solid wood suitable for the widest of my deck beams. I then shape the entire piece of wood to the camber, or curve, of the deck beam itself, and then cut thin slices off this solid piece to form the deck beams. The piece of wood has been carefully scribed down the middle to provide a centerline. FIGURE 4-7 illustrates this procedure. I cut all of the deck beams to proper length, using the centerline as a guide. Then I fasten them to the beam shelves.

Be sure to install the lower deck beams only at this point because you will need to lay the deck planks onto the beams. If you are going to install lights, this is the time to make sure the wiring is in. Templates will help you to correctly determine the shape of your deck beams while the beams are still in one piece of wood before you cut them out.

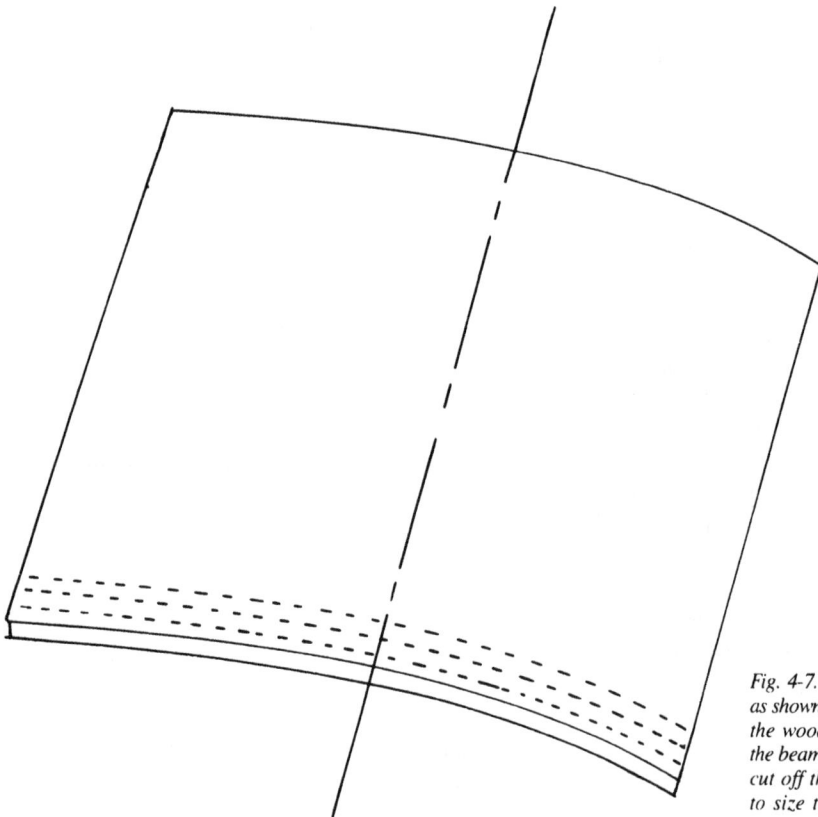

Fig. 4-7. Cut and shape a piece of wood as shown with the centerline drawn onto the wood. The dotted lines represent the beams being cut off. Once you have cut off the beams, you can trim them to size to fit their location.

You also can elect to simply carve out the shape of the deck beams on the solid hull without removing any more wood than is required, and simply install your deck planks onto the solid piece of wood. To use this method with accuracy may prove to be more difficult than you think, but again templates will play a large part in completing this step correctly. Particularly with the lower deck, it is not really necessary to make the deck beams since they will not show in any way once the deck is planked. If you have an upper deck, you can also leave the lower deck solid and plank it over. I believe that hollowing out at least the upper decks and using deck beams to plank over produces a much better effect, since you can leave some of the deck planks off to show the lower deck.

You might consider furnishing your captain's cabin and some of the other areas of your ship, which I did with my pirate brig. It was fun to do, although I will admit that it is very hard to see now, especially since the model is in a case. The neon light effect does come off very well, and helps to show to some extent what is in the captain's cabin.

PLANK-ON-BULKHEAD SHIP

I will leave the solid-hull model and turn to the next type of model, that of the plank-on-bulkhead ship kit. If this is the type you are building, then you have a false deck made out of a thin plywood supplied in the kit. You must install it prior to planking your lower deck. The planks are intended to lie over this thin plywood.

One word of extra caution here. I have found in my experience with this type of kit that the tops of the bulkheads, which are really being used for the deck beams, are not always cut out to the right height or curvature! You should carefully measure them and check at this point, or your cannon will not fit properly into your gunports for one thing. If you have marked your bulkheads as suggested in Chapter 3, it will make this part of your work a lot easier, since you have an accurate line to follow.

When you are performing these measurements, remember that you have both the thickness of the false deck plus the thickness of your planking material to consider. When I was building my model of the *Friesland*, a Dutch ship of the line by Mamoli of Italy,

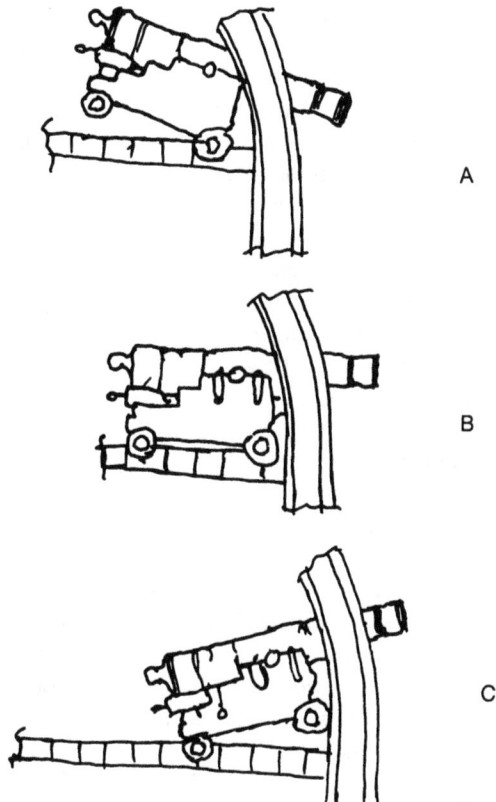

Fig. 4-8. The correct position of the deck in relation to the gunport (B), and the two errors that can occur (A) and (B) if the deck is not at the right level with the gunports.

I used a template made up of a piece of material the same thickness as the false deck supplied in the kit and planked it with some wood the same thickness as supplied in the kit. I laid the template atop three of the bulkheads, holding it down in position with my fingers. I had previously mounted several of the cannon supplied with the kit, so I put one cannon through the hull gunport to see if it fit with the deck in place (FIG. 4-8). The case where the bulkhead was still too high is illustrated in FIG. 4-8A. FIGURE 4-8B shows what it should look like, and FIG. 4-8C shows what happens if the bulkhead is too low. I checked the template with the marks I had left on my bulkheads. I had already corrected some of them prior to installation. A little more adjustment was required on two of the bulkheads, and I am glad that I checked because I had the ability to correct the problem at this point.

You will also notice that I had not yet installed the false deck, which I was told to do in the instructions prior to this time. I had fit the false deck, but then removed it once the bulkheads were braced with additional material not supplied in the kit. I then planked the hull with the first layer of planks, then coated the inside with Deft to seal the inner planks from harm while I could get at them. I next installed the false deck as indicated, while checking for the proper alignment of the gunports, which I cut out after the first layer of planking was installed. The second layer of planking then followed, following the scratch builder's techniques.

You do not have to follow the instructions supplied in the kit exactly as written, but may modify them to your own way of planking. You should use the instructions as a guide to assist you. You also may alter the exact order of kit instructional procedure after careful study if you can determine that this will make your work easier. Additions to the kit type models will only improve them, and as your experience grows, you will find that a lot of improvement can be incorporated into these kit models to make them both more accurate and more fun to build. They can be successfully built following the kit instructions, but I find it easier to follow my own modified way. Many things are left out of the kit instructions and are really learned through actually building models.

With other plank-on-bulkhead kits I have built, such as the yacht *Mary* by Mamoli and the *Le Mirage* by Corel, I did follow the instructions of the kit with good results, although I would have changed some of the things had I known what I do now. In these models, I installed the false deck first, then the deck planking, before I did the outer hull planking. One problem that might result is that you cannot check your deck locations for the simple reason that your gunports are not yet installed. As a result, you often must make some modifications to the gun carriages in order to install the cannon correctly. The following deck planking procedures should be used by both kit and scratch builders.

INTERNAL WORK

You must do some of the internal work now if you are scratch building your model. You must complete all of the internal work before you put in your deck beams, since it will be very hard to get inside this area once the deck beams are in place.

It is most important that you strengthen the sections of the hull that will support the channels for your deadeyes for the shrouds of your standing rigging, as well as the chain plates, a part of your ship model's standing rigging construction. The reason this is so important is that a lot of pressure will be applied to this part of your hull by the force of the shrouds that hold up your masts. To prepare for this force, install filling pieces of wood between the frames glued against your outer planks (FIG. 4-9). The exact position of these filling pieces of wood must be determined from your plans.

You should also put filling pieces between your beam shelf and the planking to give you something to attach your waterways to. This step is done at the deck level between the frames. You will also want to check the rest of your model to see if there is any other place where you might need additional support for external fittings, or for holes which you may have to put into your hull, such as the hawse holes where the anchor rope goes through, the scupper holes (FIGS. 4-10 and 4-11), oar ports (FIG. 4-12), and any other item you feel needs some additional support.

Do not forget to put in your *mast step*. This is simply a piece of wood with a hole cut into it that is glued and doweled to the top of the keelson. Your mast is then later installed with a peg at the bottom of it that will fit into this hole. If you want to do things absolutely correct, use a square hole, not a round one. Be aware, however, that it is much more difficult to line up the square cut than a round one. The top of the mast has a square top upon which the cap and other items fit, and this top square must match up perfectly with the bottom square or it will be a little to the port or starboard side—it will have a kind of twisted look. It helps a great deal if your beams are already made up to get the right position of the mast steps.

DECK BEAMS

This leads me to Henry Bridenbecker's next suggestion, which I have followed with great success, and that is to make your deck beams before you plank

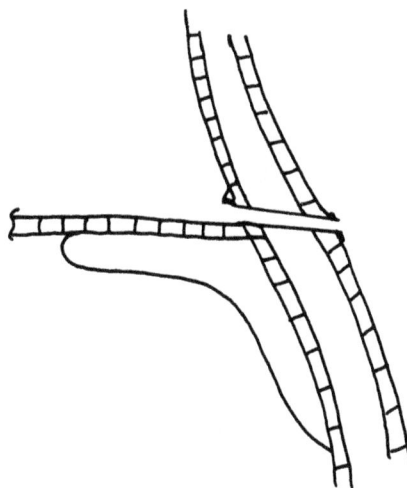

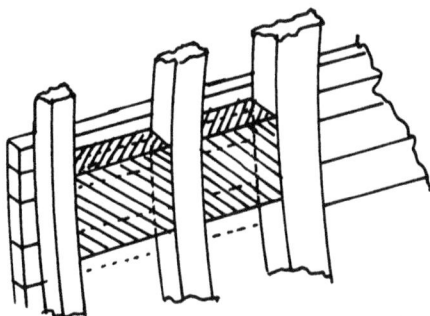

Fig. 4-9. The installation of wood backing material at the location of the chainplates. This is a good idea for the kit builder also, but you have to plan ahead in this case since you usually cannot get behind the planks once you have planked a kit model.

Fig. 4-10. A typical scupper cross section.

Fig. 4-11. Bob Graham's model of the Eagle under construction showing the scuppers installed above the wale.

your hull. Make the deck beams so that they are a tight fit, and do not glue them into position until you have planked your hull and done all of your internal work. You can, however, fit them into position to make sure your hull does not move when you plank and to give it added support. This method also helps a tremendous amount when you go to install your mast steps because it enables you to align the angle of the mast through the deck beams and the timbers that support the mast at the deck level if you locate exactly your mast step on the keelson.

You can determine this angle and the position of the mast step from the plans, but I find that the additional help of actually having the deck-beam structure there to assist is of great help. You should use the plans to determine the location of the mast step to make doubly sure you are at the right position, because once the mast step is installed and the deck is laid, you cannot go back and change it.

You now will make your beams, which can be made out of one block of wood as suggested earlier in this chapter. In addition to cutting the camber of the deck beam at the top, you also might want to cut the camber at the bottom of the beam. You can omit this latter procedure if you are going to plank the complete deck, and you can even leave it out if you are going to only leave a few planks off since it is very hard to see. If you love to construct the ship and want to build one as accurately as possible, you will want to add the camber underneath the plank.

If your plans do not tell you what this camber is, the general rule is that the rise is ¼ inch per foot, which means that every ¼ inch of rise in the center of the beam from the level beam is gained for every foot of length of the beam. Check this out with calculations against what is given you in your plans.

This brings up another point on plans; that is, some plans do not always match each other! What I mean is that the body plan might be off from the sheer plan by as much as ¹⁄₁₆ inch. If you have already done your frames and planking, you have already found out this problem. You will need to redraw some of your plans to correct for this error.

You should also check all beam plans, which you will receive with a good set of plans from some sources, to make sure they are in line with the other plans

Fig. 4-12. Dick Roos' model of the H.M.S. Peregrine Galley, *based on a Sergal plank-on-bulkhead kit but with many scratch modifications. Notice the oar ports just above the wale between the gunports.*

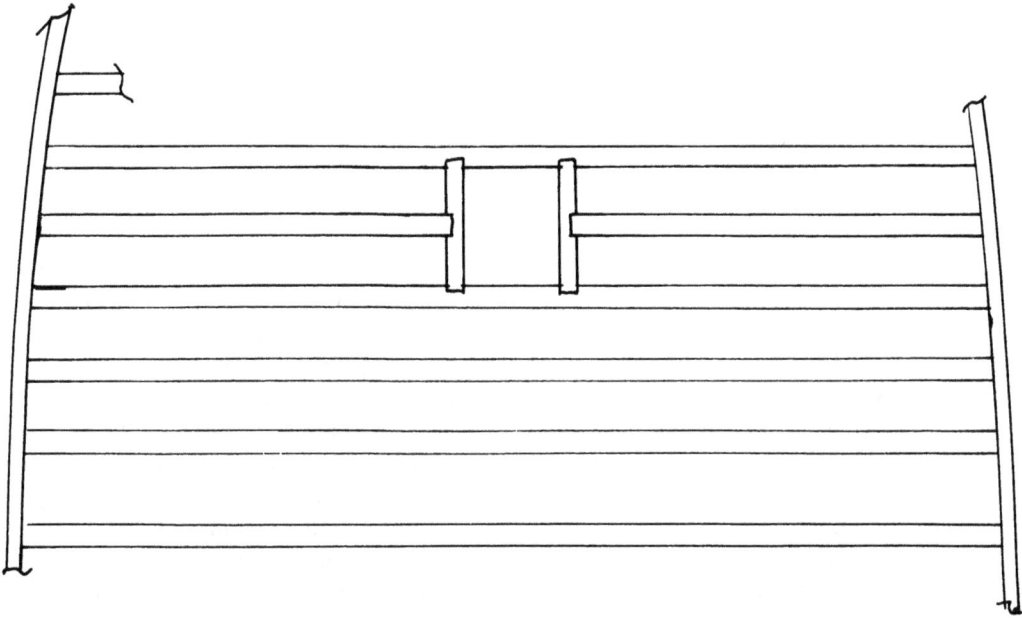

Fig. 4-13. The basic deck skeleton structure without all of the details added. If you are going to fully plank your deck, then this is all you will need in the way of a structure.

Fig. 4-14. Ed Marple's Conqueror *with the upper deck beams and carlings in place.* (Photo courtesy of Ed Marple.)

already used and of the same scale. A typical deck "skeleton" with all the deck beams, hatch carlings, and mast partners is shown in FIG. 4-13.

Ed Marple's model of the *Conqueror* is shown in FIG. 4-14 with the upper deck beams installed and ready for planking. Notice that all of the work on the lower deck has already been completed.

Make all of the deck beams at the same time with the same camber, and then form-fit each beam to its location and number or identify it in some way as to exactly which beam it is. The best way to make these beams is to start from the midship beam and work your way forward and aft, fitting as you go.

It is hard enough to make the beams themselves first, without complicating procedures by trying to make all of the fore and aft carlings or timbers and the other items, such as the mast partners, at the same time. First you should make all of the deck beams and make them to go all the way across the ship from port to starboard. After all of the deck beams are fully formed and fitted, then you can make the other timbers and cut the already-made beams carefully to fit as required.

The beams do not only have a camber, they must also follow the sheer of the ship. Look at your half-breadth plan or the side view of the ship. Here you will again see that the deck does not follow the waterline of the ship, but follows the sheer of the hull. This means that the beams must also follow this sheer. At the midship area, this sheer will be nearly flat, which will make the beams nearly flat. At the bow and stern, however, the sheer of the deck will not be flat and you must cut or sand the deck beams to this slope. In addition, you must cut the ends of the deck beams to the proper angle to fit the side of the ship as they rest atop the beam shelf.

A view of the *Sovereign of the Seas* under construction by Ed Marple shows the sheer from the outside of the hull (FIG. 4-15). FIGURE 4-16 shows the beam shelf, which follows the sheer of the ship, with the deck beam atop it.

The first thing you must do once you have cut out the rough deck beams is to draw a line on the frames of your ship just where the deck line is located. Remember, you drew the waterline onto your frames much earlier. Here is one time when the drawn waterline will become invaluable. From your plans, measure from this waterline to the sheer of your deck or your deck line from the waterline plan, which is the side view of your ship. Carefully take

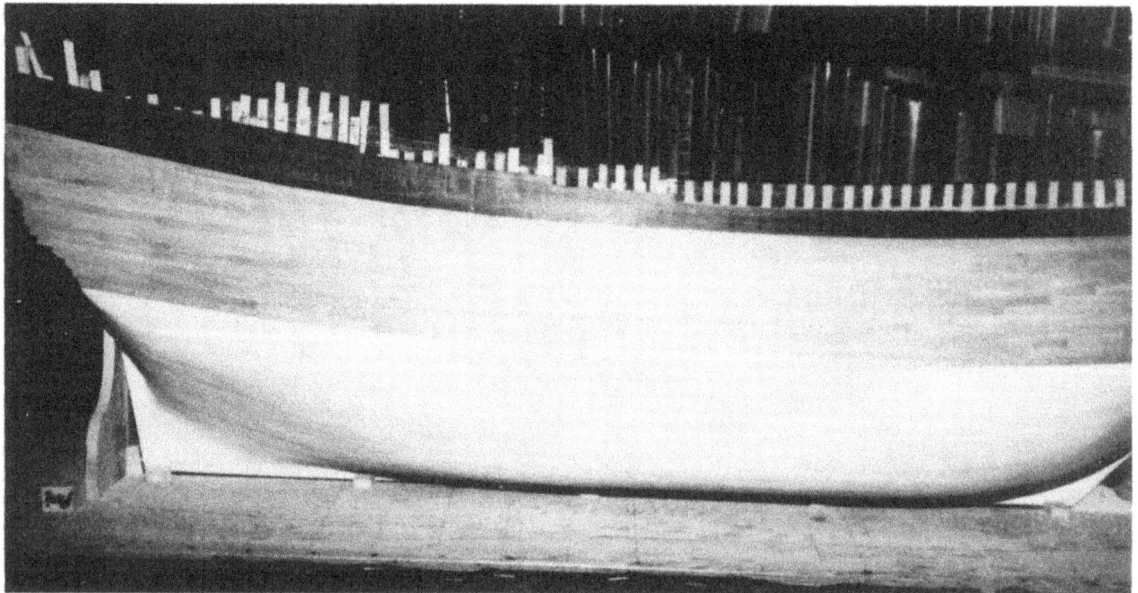

Fig. 4-15. The H.M.S. Sovereign of the Seas *by Ed Marple under construction, showing the sheer of the vessel from the outer hull. Also note the three different types of wood used to plank the hull.* (Photo courtesy of Ed Marple.)

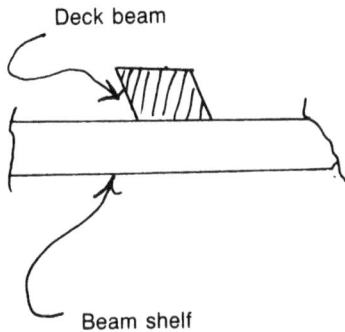

Fig. 4-16. The cross section of the deck beam lying on the beam shelf, showing the camber you must put on the bottom as well as the top of the deck beam in order to achieve a flat surface for the installation of your deck planks.

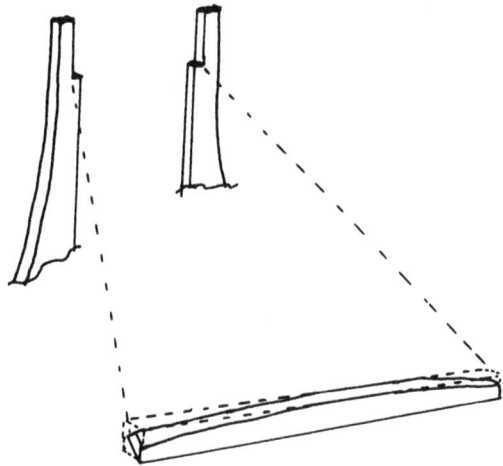

Fig. 4-17. An example of fitting a deck beam when constructing a plank-on-bulkhead kit model. Do not forget to put the correct camber onto the beam.

each of these measurements and transfer them to your ship, thus giving you a line to follow on your ship. You will have already done this procedure if you have already installed your beam shelf.

In the case of a multidecked vessel, you will have more beam shelves to install on your ship. Lay your rough beam in place and measure the cut to fit the beam length at the midship location. Cut the ends off of the beam, leaving a little extra to form-fit the beam. Using sandpaper on a sanding disk or by hand, finish the ends of the deck beam until it fits properly, lying flat on the beam shelf and fitting snugly against both sides of the hull. Using the line you have just drawn to represent the bottom of the deck, now mark the thickness of the beam. You have already cut out the beam camber, and it should come very close if not right on to the drawn line. Remember that the curve shown on the plans runs at the top of the deck. FIGURE 4-17 depicts the beam being cut and fit into place.

You should mark the sheer line on each side of the deck beam. When you begin to notice a difference in the level of this mark on the sides of the deck beam, then you must make a bevel in the deck beam much like you made in your frames around the bow and stern areas. The bevel on the deck beam is marked by the marks you make on the end of the beams. This bevel in the beam will be the way the deck planks will run when you come to plank the deck. If the bevel is not put into the deck beam, then the deck plank will only rest upon the corner of the deck beam and will be difficult to dowel in properly.

You must also take into account this bevel of the deck sheer at the bottom of the deck beam, since it rests on the beam shelf, which itself is following the sheer of the deck. Do not forget to cut this angle into the bottom of the beam before you measure the top cut, or you will ruin the beam.

It might seem like unnecessary work at this point to get the deck beams correctly in place, but it will save you a lot of trouble when you install your deck planks. Make sure when making your deck beams that both sides of the centerline you marked on your beam are equal. The center of your beam must be in the center of your ship model's deck.

Lodging Knees

The *lodging knees* can be made now. If you are building a kit and have made your deck beams much the same as the scratch builder, you will use this same procedure. Try to do the best job you can. If you want to leave some deck beams exposed, you must do it correctly. The lodging knees are pieces of wood that act as supports for the beams (FIG. 4-18). You can mass-produce them by forming them in one piece of wood (FIG. 4-19), then cutting them out as required. For this operation, a good hardwood must be used, such as alder, pear, or boxwood.

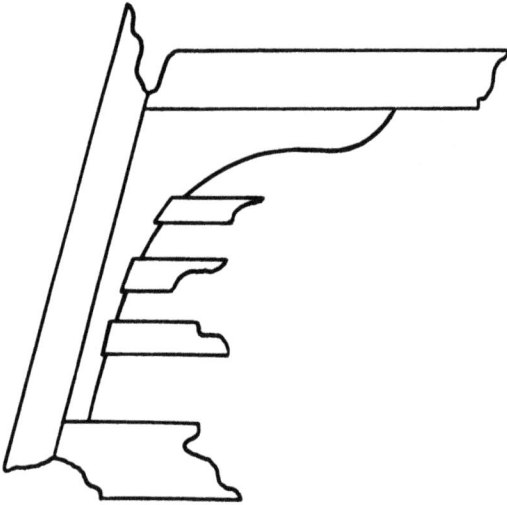

Fig. 4-18. A typical example of a lodging knee installed between deck beams and against the bulkhead.

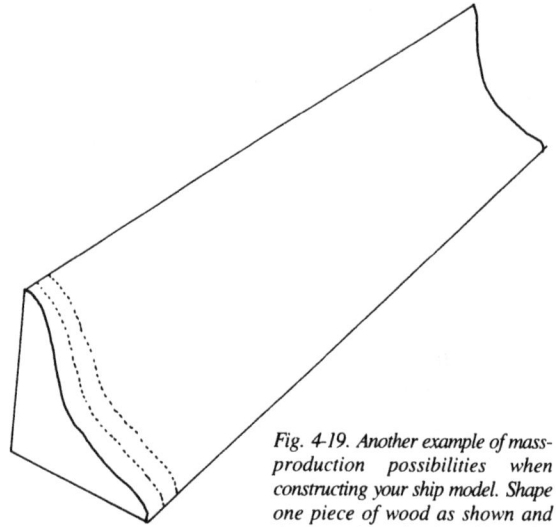

Fig. 4-19. Another example of mass-production possibilities when constructing your ship model. Shape one piece of wood as shown and then cut along the dotted lines for each lodging knee as required. You will need many of them.

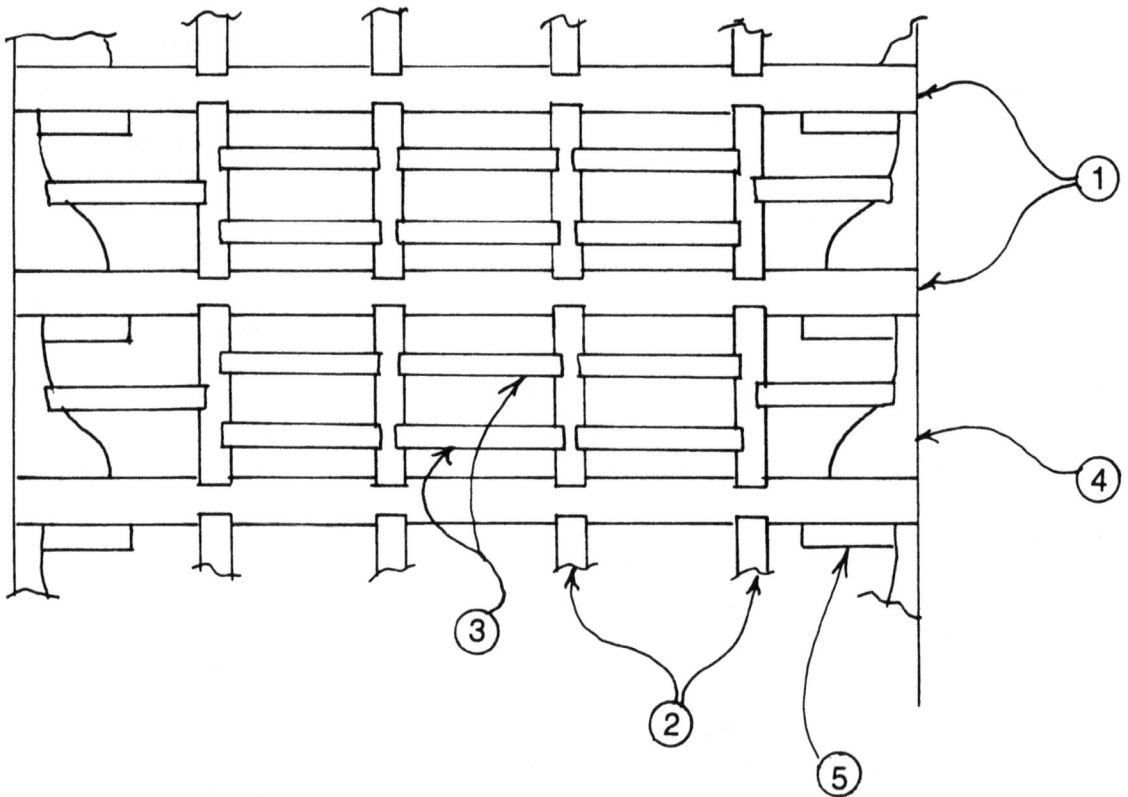

Fig. 4-20. A view of a fully detailed deck structure: 1. the deck beam, 2. the carlings, 3. the ledges, 4. the lodging knee, and 5. the hanging knee.

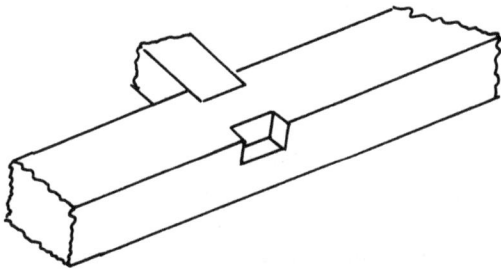

Fig. 4-21. An example of the mortice cut into the deck beam to accept the carling piece.

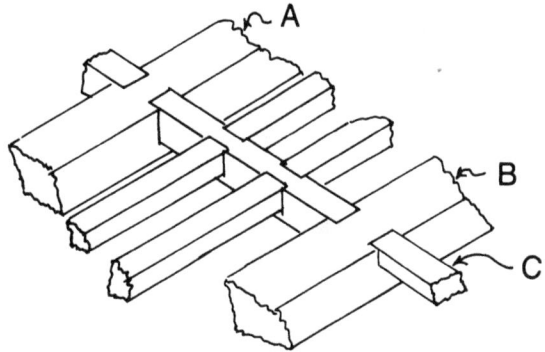

Fig. 4-22. Deck beam A is slightly higher than deck beam B, which means that carling C must be shaped accordingly. The deck will be installed over all of this, and all parts of the deck structure should make contact with the deck plank, but not pull or push the plank out of its proper level position.

Carlings

The next step is to fit all of the beams and determine where to place the carlings and which deck beams to cut and where. This is an exercise in careful wood joinery. You can make the carlings up of two to six rows from fore to aft of timber, depending on the size of the ship and how many you want to install. There are side tier carlings, middle tier carlings, and carlings next to the middle line (FIG. 4-20). FIGURE 4-20 also shows the lodging knee in place, as well as the hanging knee and the ledges between the beams.

If you want to follow the practice of the actual ship construction, install all of these timbers. Many models install only the beams and carlings, which are absolutely necessary for the hatches, along with some lodging knees. If you are going to plank most or all of your deck, then it is not necessary for you to install all of these timbers. If you are going to install little or no deck planking, you should install all of the timbers you can.

You will require a carling at the main hatch, for example, so I will describe the procedure for its installation. Locate the beam that will be at the fore part of the hatch, and carefully mark the position of the hatch from your plans onto the deck beam. After you have marked this deck beam, remove it from the ship and carefully cut a mortice into the beam where the carling will fit into it. Do this on both the port and starboard side, as shown in FIG. 4-21. Henry Bridenbecker suggests using a very thin X-ACTO blade or Uber knife for these types of cuts when fitting the carlings.

Now replace the deck beam into its proper position and go to the aft deck beam of the main hatch. Mark this beam where the carling will fit into it. Remove this beam and again cut two mortices into it where the carling will be installed. Install this beam back into the ship model, and remove all deck beams in between the fore and aft ends of the main hatch.

Take a piece of wood the same size as your deck beams and cut it to make your carling. Two will be needed. You should cut the carling a little bit longer than you actually need so that you can carefully sand-fit it in between the two deck beams you just morticed without bending them. Also make sure that you follow any sheer that is in the deck at that point. FIGURE 4-22 shows an example of the sheer problem and what should be considered when forming this carling. I do not think you will have much of a problem with the main hatch, since there is very little sheer in the middle of the ship. You will have to watch this when you come to the ends of the ship model.

The carlings when finished should fit in between the two deck beams with no force, but be snug enough so that they will stay in place before gluing.

The next step is to lay the deck beams you re-moved back down over the carlings, which are now across the deck beams' path. Carefully mark where each deck beam crosses the carling on both the port and starboard side. Mark the deck beam at the same time. Remove the carlings and carefully cut mortices into them for the deck beams you have just marked. Then take the deck beams and cut them to fit into the carlings after you have reinstalled the carlings onto the ship. These deck beams will now become your *half-beams;* they will go from the frame to the carling and not from frame to frame. FIGURE 4-20 shows the half-beams, carlings, deck beams, etc.

Once you have made the carlings and half-beams for the main hatch, remove them and install the fore and aft deck beam only with the mortices already cut. Put glue on the ends of the carlings and install them into the deck beams at the mortices. Then put glue on the inside edge of the half-beams and glue them to the mortices cut into the carlings. Do not glue the ends of the beams to the frames yet. When you are happy with the location of all of the beams in this assembly, set them aside to dry before going any further. After they are dry, you can remove the glued assembly from its location and dowel all of the joints made with your wooden dowels.

In this way, you can install all of your carlings, advancing one beam at a time, until you come to another hatch or to where your mast will be placed, then install them in much the same manner as just described. With the individual beams, each carling will be morticed into both beams.

Ledges

You can now decide if you will need any ledges in your deck structure. If your ship is a large warship, I would think that they would be installed. You also might be one of the very fortunate modelers to have an accurate set of plans from a reliable source, such as a museum, showing all of the details of the deck. You could do no better than to follow these plans.

You might well wonder if all of this work is worth the effort. It all depends on you and what you want to do. In all of this work, be sure that you do as clean and accurate a job of it as you can. The craftsmanship of your model will be judged on both the quality and the quantity of work. You are the sole judge on all of these matters. The main goal is for you to have fun and enjoy your labor of love. If the ship model is built correctly, your efforts will be admired for a long time to come. It comes as an added benefit that your model is also much stronger if built correctly.

Leaving a few planks off the deck, just like leaving them off the hull to show your frames, isn't incorrect. The choice is up to you.

When all deck beams are completed, glue and dowel them to the frames and the beam shelves. Before you do, consider painting the inside of your hull with Deft or some such wood sealing substance. Do not use anything that leaves the wood with a glossy look, since this is not the way things looked in the old days, and is apt to give the model a "toy" look.

Apply a flat, clear finish to the wood to protect it from the elements and preserve your work for as long as possible. I have seen pictures of some of the admiralty models that have been damaged by rot and decay and by the wood termite. To see such damage to such beautiful models is hard to accept. Avoiding this fate for your model is easy to do and does not take much time.

DECK PLANKING

You have now arrived at the part of the process that is the most fun for many modelers: doing the deck work. You must do the lower deck, if there is one, before the upper deck on your vessel, and you will put the deck beams in for your lower deck and plank it before putting in your deck beams for any of the upper decks. You must also seal the underside of your decks before you glue and dowel them into place, since it is very difficult to seal them after they have been glued down.

FIGURE 3-20 shows Ed Marple's model of the *Conqueror* with the lowest deck beams in place and part of the deck already installed. Ed next installed the middle deck, which is shown in FIG. 4-23. FIGURE 4-14 shows the next step, which is the installation of the beams for the upper deck. The sequence continues with FIG. 4-24 showing the upper deck completely rigged with the poop deck beams in place. FIGURE 4-25 is a picture of Ed's completed deck work with final details yet to be added.

Notice that Ed Marple, even though he uses deck beams, etc., does not leave any of his planking undone.

Kits

If you are a kit builder and have elected not to install deck beams on your ship, a great help in laying

Fig. 4-23. *The upper gun deck of the* Conqueror *showing the details of the gun installations. All work on the deck must be completed before the next deck can be installed.* (Photo courtesy of Ed Marple.)

Fig. 4-24. *The quarter deck and forecastle deck are the next decks to be installed, as shown in this photograph of the* Conqueror *by Ed Marple.* (Photo courtesy of Ed Marple.)

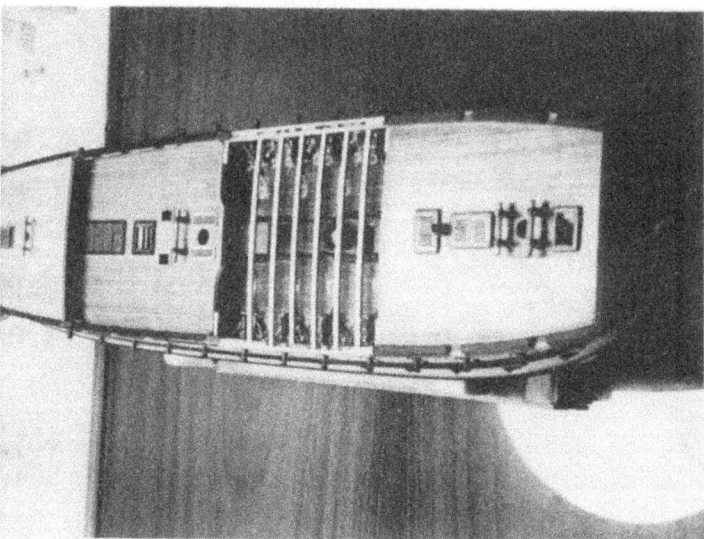

Fig. 4-25. *The* Conqueror, *showing the final stages of the upper deck installation.* (Photo courtesy of Ed Marple.)

out your deck is to draw on your false deck the location of the centers of your beams before you install the false deck. These marks will provide you with a guide for laying your planks. I have found that you can even go to the extent of drawing in your planks on your false deck with the butts laid out. In this way, you can correct any error in your work before you even begin to lay the planks, and all you have to do when you get to this point is to cut and fit your planks.

Generally, the deck planking was not as wide as the planking used for your ship's hull. It was not always the same material, either. One of the best woods to use for your deck is holly, which is a white wood. In any case, you should use a light-colored wood for your deck, since most of the ships of this period were *hollystoned,* or rubbed with flat sand stones to make them as white as possible.

As an added help to kit builders, it has been my experience that the material supplied in the kit for planking the deck is very difficult to work with, and warps and splits at the most inopportune time. I suggest that you obtain some of your own wood for this purpose and discard the kit wood. I, for one, will never use the kit supplied deck planking material again. I find it much more satisfactory to use a good wood such as holly. You can plank a deck with kit-supplied material, however (FIG. 4-26).

Caulking

The caulking seams of the planks can be done in a variety of ways, but the method that has evolved with the Ship Modelers Association members is to use a dark pencil to mark the edges of the planks. The pencil should be a number H or even F, which is a very soft lead and leaves a heavy, dark line along the edge of the plank.

That is not the only method. I have used black

Fig. 4-26. My model of the yacht Mary, *showing the deck fully planked using material supplied in the kit.*

markers successfully to mark in the caulking, and some of the modelers have used black paper and dark photo negatives to accomplish the same purpose. Some modelers use nothing at all. It depends on your personal choice.

If you are not sure what you want to use, then try several different methods, first marking the edge of several planks and then laying them down on a separate board or piece of paper to see what they will look like. For the paper and photo negative methods, glue the black material on the edge of a number of planks held together with a clamp and then cut them apart with a razor blade. The soft pencil lead and black marker pen methods can be done plank by plank as you go, or mass-produced as indicated with the paper method. All methods have been used by modelers with success.

Blacken only one edge of the plank, and lay the black side against a white or clean side of the next deck plank. This caulked line should not be too obvious. FIGURE 4-27 is a good example of a deck well done by another fine modeler of the S.M.A., Tom Palen.

Plank Dimensions

The deck planks on a real ship were cut as long as possible, since they did not have all of the problems associated with the hull planking. The deck planks varied in width, depending on the period the ship was constructed. Generally, the planks tended to become narrower as time progressed. The largest width was in the sixteenth century, and was about 18 inches maximum. In the seventeenth century, this maximum width was about 15 inches, then it went down to 14 inches in the eighteenth century, while by the nineteenth century it had reduced to about 8 inches.

It took a long time for the ship-building industry to accept the fact that wider planks have a greater tendency to warp and twist than do narrower planks on the deck. FIGURE 4-28 shows a modern deck on a ship model, which indicates the narrow modern deck. I would say that deck planks about 12 inches wide would be about 3/16 wide on a 3/16-inch-scale model and would be about right for most of your models from the sixteenth century up to about the end of the eighteenth century. This size of deck planking would give you the doweling pattern indicated in FIG. 4-29.

King Plank

After establishing the plank width and maximum length, the first plank you will install is the plank that

Fig. 4-27. An example of a deck done by scratch on what was originally a plank-on-bulkhead kit of the model H.M.S. Endeavour by Tom Palen. Notice the correct scale gratings, which Tom worked very hard on.

Fig. 4-28. The interior of the White Wings II *by Rolly Kalajian. Notice how thin the deck planks are. The detail and furniture, all scratch, speak for themselves.*

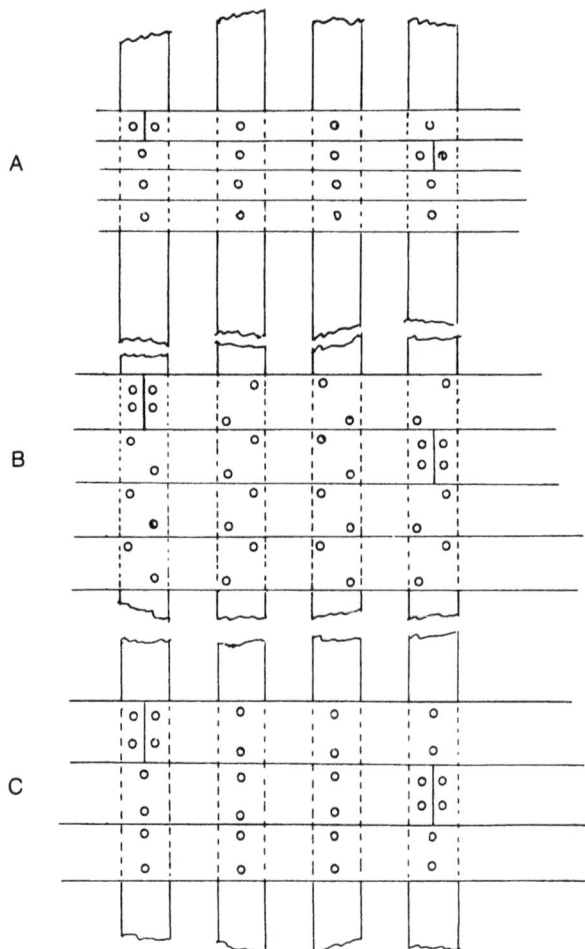

Fig. 4-29. The rule for doweling planks. If planks are less than 6 inches in width, then A *is the pattern to use. If the planks are between 6 and 11 inches, then pattern* B *should be used. Pattern* C *is for planks wider than 11 inches.*

will go down the middle of the deck, sometimes referred to as the *king plank*. This plank will run into the hatches and mast locations, as well as any other obstruction down the middle of your deck.

It should run right down the middle of your deck, with its center matching the centerline you drew on the beams or on the false deck, which you have already installed. If you are building a kit model, then you are installing these planks on the false deck. If you are scratch building a plank-on-frame model, you will install these deck planks on your beams.

There is a third option to follow, and this is to install a false deck on the beams before installing your planks. In this way, you do not need to install as many beams and all the details of the deck beam structure. It will require you to plank the entire deck. You will not have to worry about the slight imperfections of the deck beam making it difficult to install your deck planks, but you must take into account the extra thickness of this false deck if you opt for this method. Ed Marple's model of the *Prince* shows the installation of the upper deck in progress (FIG. 4-30).

Lay the plank itself in pieces. Take the deck planking material and carefully measure the distance with the plank between the aft hatch and the stern counter. It really makes no difference where you start with this deck plank as long as it is the middle plank. It must be run completely from fore to aft. Check to make sure that it does divide the deck neatly into two halves. When you have completed your deck planking, it should be the same on both sides with the same number of planks running fore to aft on both sides, much the same as with the hull.

Both sides of this plank should have the soft pencil line drawn on it to represent the caulking of the seams. The rest of your planks will have one side only marked.

Take the first plank carefully measured between the parts indicated and glue and dowel it down to the deck beams or false deck. The false deck should have marks to indicate the beams so that you can accurately install the dowels. Nothing looks worse on a deck than to see the dowel line formed across the deck wander all over the place. FIGURE 4-31 is a good example of what the deck should look like.

Do not try to hurry this part of your project. The

Fig. 4-30. Ed Marple's H.M.S. Prince *under construction. Ed was not happy with the poop deck installation and is removing and reinstalling some of the planks.* (Photo courtesy of Ed Marple.)

deck is one of the most visible areas, and one that most people look at. Neatness with the deck is a must.

The scribed decking provided in most of the solid-hull kits is to me more trouble than it is worth. It can be used and will speed up the process of planking your deck if this is your desire. I think that the satisfaction gained from laying your own deck, and the result is worth much more than the small amount of time saved. If you have already improved your solid-hull model by planking the outside of the hull, why would you not want to also plank the deck?

Other Deck Planks

Once you have laid the king deck planks, you will proceed to install the rest of the deck planks, much the same way you did your hull. Lay one plank to the port side of the king plank and then lay its duplicate on the starboard side. You can make two planks at a time, one for the port and one for the starboard side. Work out from the center, always laying the deck planks with the dark, marked side against the light, unmarked side.

Before completing the deck planking, make sure that you have installed all of the required structures on the deck-beam structure. Any bits, braces, or other items such as the capstan post and mast partners must be in place before you install the deck. A careful study of your plans will save you much trouble in the future.

Butts

The placing of the butts of the planking must be done carefully, but if you have already planned the spacing as suggested earlier you will have no problem. The butts on the port side should match those on the starboard side. The size of the dowels that will be used should be determined by the scale of your ship model. The dowel or treenail was about 1 to 1½ inches in diameter. If you are fortunate enough to have accurate plans of your ship, you will also know if you should use copper or iron nails along with your treenails. Using the drawplate to make dowels or treenails down to about a #75 size drill and making the holes one size larger, a #74, is about right for a 1:16 scale model or your average 1:75 scale kit model.

Margin Plank

Before you run any of the deck planks into the bulwarks or walls of your ship, you might need to

Fig. 4-31. Henry Bridenbecker's model of a Colonial bark (1640) showing deck details and the clean run of the deck doweling.

install a margin plank. Install the *margin plank* first because it is much easier than trying to cut it in later. The margin plank is the plank that runs along the edge of the bulwark and is usually a little wider than the rest of the planking.

In the Dutch and English ships, the fore part of the deck planking is *joggled* into the margin plank. This was not true for all ships, so you will have to check your plans carefully. If your plans indicate that this was the case, you should install the deck planks at the bow in this way. FIGURE 4-32 shows some methods of joggling the deck planks.

As in all areas of ship model construction, you must follow the rules for this procedure. The rule for joggling the planks is that the angle cut for the margin plank cannot be more than twice the width of the plank. If it exceeds this limit, it must be joggled into the margin plank, which means the end must be cut flat, as shown in FIG. 4-32. The flat end should not be more than roughly one-half of the plank's width.

To be fully correct, the *waterway* is the piece of timber that comes between the margin plank and the bulkhead. In other words, proceed from the deck planks to the margin plank to the waterway timber then to the bulwark or wall of the ship. Your plans should indicate just what is required. FIGURE 4-33 shows this arrangement to the best advantage.

Removing the Bulkheads

If you are a plank-on-bulkhead kit builder, you must remove the top parts of your bulkheads as indicated in the kit instructions. An option you can consider is to remove only part of the top of the bulkhead (FIG. 4-34).

This is one of the areas in which some of the kit instructions can give you a real problem. The kit instructs you to lay the deck prior to planking the hull. You cannot completely lay down the deck planking because the top part of the bulkhead frame cannot be removed before you plank the outside of the hull. You should also install the margin plank along with the waterway if the deck is to be done in the right way.

There is no reason why you cannot modify the directions of the kit in order to compensate for this fact. You can lay the deck planks at almost any time you wish, and you should really wait until after you

have completed the hull planking. This also enables you to better locate the proper positions for your upper gunports which, as indicated earlier, can be a problem when you have to install your cannon if they are not located properly. This is no problem if your model has no gunports, but even so I believe that it is much better to plank your hull first and then plank your deck.

Covering Board

FIGURE 4-34 also shows additions to the already installed upper portions of the bulkhead that simulate the frames which are not there as well as add strength to the hull planking in this area. In many ships, they were planked over with the bulwark inside, or planked over with ceiling planking, but some ships did not. If this is the case with your model and it is a kit type, then remove all of the upper portion of the frame, sand it smooth with the false deck, and install false bulwark stanchions before installing the covering board, which you should notch to take the bulwark stanchions.

The covering board (FIG. 4-33) is usually installed on merchant ships, which do not generally have the bulwarks planked. Warships usually do have their bulwarks planked (FIG. 4-35). The bulwark construction depends on which deck is being discussed.

The decks shown in FIGS. 4-33 and 4-35 are *weather decks,* or decks that are exposed to the elements. The lower decks of the seventeenth and eighteenth centuries also had waterways much like the weather decks. Construction of the lower deck bulwarks and deck planking changed from about the mid-eighteenth century, so you should have a good set of plans to follow if you are building one of these models. If you have any doubt as to which procedure to follow, then follow your plans or the kit instructions only. Again, it is better to not put in a detail if you are not sure of its accuracy, than to put in an extra detail on your ship model only to find out later that it is incorrect.

Getting back to deck planking, you have now installed the deck, the margin plank, and/or the waterway, depending on the type of ship you are building. Many times the waterway and the margin plank were the same plank. With some of the ships,

Snipe

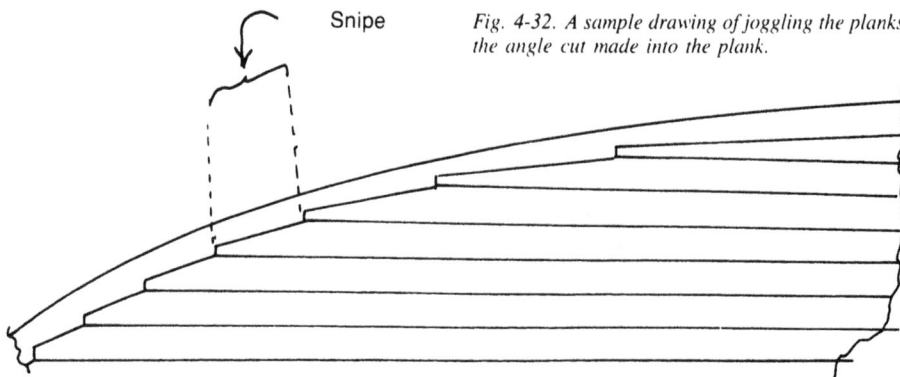

Fig. 4-32. A sample drawing of joggling the planks. The snipe is the angle cut made into the plank.

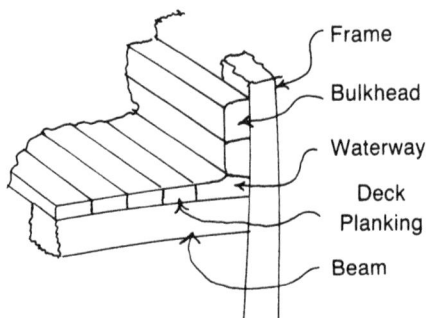

Fig. 4-33. A basic deck structure.

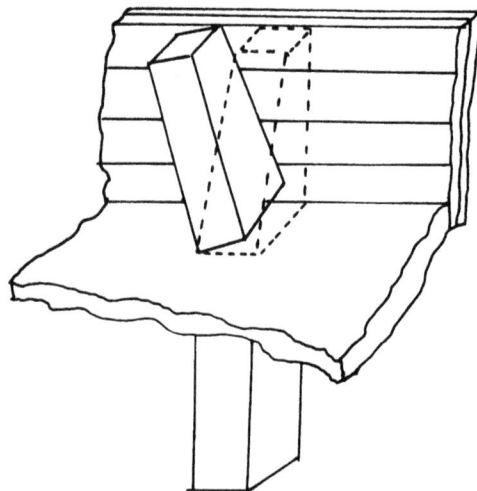

Frame
Bulkhead
Waterway
Deck
Planking
Beam

Fig. 4-34. Removing the top part of the bulkhead on the plank-on-bulkhead kits to install the deck planking.

the covering board covered the ends of the planks and there was no waterway.

This last design is the easiest type of ship to build as far as the deck planking is concerned. You can run the deck planks right up to the edge of the bulwark and install the covering board over the deck planking. You still must notch the covering board or cut it in to fit between the bulwark stanchions. The best way to cut the covering board so that it will fit properly is to use templates. I cannot stress enough how much time and wood you will save if you make cardboard templates.

Before you install your covering board or begin to install the bulwark planking, you should clean up and sand down your deck planks, which you have just laid. This would include your margin plank

and/or waterway piece. Do not polish the deck or give it a glossy look in any way. Can you imagine what a polished deck would be like on a real ship in a heavy sea? Use a good coat of Deft on the deck at this time in your construction, since it will help keep both the deck planking clean and make for easy cleanup if something is spilled on the deck at a later date.

The covering board is made up much like in real life, with a number of pieces about the same length as the deck planks. Use cardboard templates first, carefully cutting them out to fit into the stanchions. The bow area will be one of the most difficult sections to make, and you should use great care in obtaining the right cuts so that the fit is just right. Do not be concerned about discarding your template if it does not fit just right. You can use the template that you have made a mistake on to make the second template, stopping at the point where you made the mistake. Once the template is made and it fits just right, turn it over and try the template on the other side of the hull. It should fit neatly on the other side, if both sides of your hull are identical, as they should be. If not, you must make another template for that side. Once the template is made, cut the covering board out of the material you have chosen for this purpose.

With a kit model, you will have to supply your own wood to make any additions to your model that are not indicated in your plans. I have yet to see a kit model that tells you to make covering boards, waterways, or any of the small details to the deck that should be there.

Some of the plank-on-bulkhead kits do give you these details in one or more of their plans; most do not. Added research will probably be required for most plank-on-bulkhead kit models if you want to add these deck details to your model. Consult the Sources at the end of this book, and sometimes the ship kit itself will give you hints as to where to find additional information. As an example, the plans for the Arkit model of the *Baltik,* an American colonial schooner, are lacking in any detail in many areas, including the deck. The manufacturer does tell you that these plans are based on some ship plans received from a specific museum in the United States, and that this ship can also be the *Sultana,* the *Halifax,* or the *Chauser,* and that you can simply pick the name of the ship that you want. I would strongly suggest, if you have this type of kit, to contact the museum indicated and ask for more details. You can also consult some books, in this case Howard I. Chapelle's *The Search For Speed Under Sail* and the book by Harold Hahn on his techniques of ship modeling, which specifically talk about some of these ships.

You will find as you proceed in this hobby that your level of skill will increase as you build more models, and that you will also want more details. Adding these details to a kit model can only improve your work if done correctly and will eventually lead you to scratch building.

I would also like to add that my comment

Fig. 4-35. Dick Roos' model under construction of the Lexington *by Aeropiccola. A lot of scratch effort has gone into this model, including the inner bulkheads which are planked. This is an excellent example of what can be done with a kit model by adding details.*

regarding the poor accuracy of kit plans does not extend to all plank-on-bulkhead kit models and many solid-hull models. Some of the plans by Euro Models of Italy are excellent, as are some of the plans by the solid-hull company, Model Shipways of Bogota, N.J., to name but two.

Bulwarks

I will not go into the many other details of the deck fittings and furniture since this is beyond the scope of this text. My main concern is planking and the associated items that must be discussed to complete the planking. The bulwark planking will be your next project. There might be some things that will be better done now before you plank the bulwarks. A careful study of the plans will reveal them.

The actual planking of the bulwarks really follows the same basic formula used for the hull planking. You will again plank on one side of the hull, then repeat the plank on the other side of the hull before going on to the next plank. Start at the bow area, laying the plank against the covering board or the waterway.

The bulwark plank should be no longer than the rest of your planks. In ³⁄₁₆-inch scale, a board of 4½ inches in length is again about your maximum. You will want to watch the thickness of your planks because they might vary according to the plans of your ship. As an example, warships usually had thicker planking for the first two or three planks above the waterway, which was called the *spirketing*. Sometimes this was all of the bulwark planking that existed, and the *plank sheer,* a type of covering board or rail, was installed atop this, and in turn topped by the rail, with the timberheads acting as posts or supports.

Study the plans of the ship you are in the process of building to determine the need for the inner bulwark planking. Many of the eighteenth-century merchant ships had no inner bulwark planking, but showed only the bare bulwark stanchions, which are the very tops of your ship's frames.

Proceed with the planking of the bulwarks one plank above the other until you have reached the top of the stanchions. You might need to trim this last plank a little bit to match the top of the stanchions and the outer planking.

If you are building a ship that has more than one deck level that must be taken care of, you must do the lower deck first. Install your bulwark planking as indicated previously, then proceed to your second deck planking, followed by the next series of bulwark planking.

Once an upper deck is planked, it is very difficult to go back and plank the lower deck or add anything to it. Careful planning and studying of your plans will help you to avoid any real problem. This also applies to the kit builder. Take another look at FIGS. 4-23 through 4-25 as an example of these cautions.

Planking the Stern

The stern area has not been covered yet and will be done now. The simple stern of a merchantman is not too much of a problem. It consists of installation of your planks working from the top of the *transom,* which is the back of the ship, down to the counter or curve of the back of the ship where the hull planks have terminated. On some ships, you must place these stern timbers after you have installed the hull planking, and they cover the ends of the hull planking at the stern. On other ships, you must install the stern timbers first because the hull timbers are exposed from the stern. Finally, on some ships it makes no real difference which is done first since the counter area will be covered up with moldings and/or ornamentation.

The stern areas, particularly in the seventeenth and eighteenth centuries, were often very heavily decorated with carved garlands and figures (FIGS. 4-36 and 4-37). Although it has nothing to do with planking, the ornamentation is one of the areas of the ship model that is most attractive to the novice ship model builder in particular, in the purchase of plank-on-bulkhead kits.

The inclusion in these kits of the already formed figures is a big selling point, but you can carve your own figures. If you have successfully built a large three-decker ship model from a plank-on-bulkhead kit, you can carve your own figures. By the same token, if you have built a large plastic sailing ship model, you can successfully build a wooden plank-on-frame ship model. You will also find that your skill will increase as you go along. I have followed this same path myself, starting from plastic ship model kits.

Plank the stern and bow areas much like you did the hull if this is required before you apply any of the fancy work. This will depend on the type of model you are building. A merchant ship had very little decoration. A warship, depending on the period and the size of the ship, might have had extensive decoration, or it might have been rather plain (FIG. 4-38). If you are building a Dutch model, you might encounter clinker-type planking on the upper part of the hull at the fore and aft area, but this type of planking has been covered already and should pose no problem.

Scuppers

There are a few details I would like to mention before we get into the final chapter. When you are installing the waterways around the hull, make provisions for the *scuppers*. The scuppers are little holes in the waterway that go through the hull and the outer planking. The purpose for these little holes is to let the water that comes up over the deck go back into the sea. That is also the main reason for the curve to the deck—so that the water will run to the sides of the ship and thus go back out through the scuppers.

To be perfectly correct, these scuppers should be lead lined, so insert aluminium tubing of the right

Fig. 4-36. The stern of my Le Mirage plank-on-bulkhead kit by Corel.

Fig. 4-37. The stern of my model Friesland under construction. This is a Mamoli plank-on-frame kit. Among other things, the stern has been gold leafed.

size—available from your local hobby shop—into the predrilled hole. Location points for the scuppers should be indicated in your plans. They were usually located at about the midship area since this is the lowest point of the ship's deck. If your plans do not include them, then two or three at the midpoint of your ship would be about right (FIG. 4-39). The scuppers were located on the upper deck of most ships. The larger ships had additional scuppers on the middle deck.

FIGURE 4-40 shows a typical scupper. The outside of the scupper was sometimes covered with a piece of leather or some other device to keep the water from coming back in.

Jig for Gunports

There is a jig I have used very successfully to help make all of my gunports exactly the same size while I was planking. You can use this jig on both kit and scratch models. It is simply a block of wood with a square notch cut into it at the fore end to fit into the frame of the gunport. This jig is used to make both the frame for the gunport and then to lay the planks up to the gunport, while leaving the square groove between the plank and the gunport frame (FIG. 4-41). It was always a problem to later try to frame the gunport properly until I came up with this solution.

The jig is simple to make and saves a lot of time later on. It also ensures that all of your gunports will be the same size (FIG. 4-42). If you are building a large three decker, you will need to make one of these jigs for each of the rows of gunports, since they will vary in size.

You also can use this jig to make the gunports themselves by using it as a template. Lay the front portion of the jig against the stock to be used for the inner face of the gunport and trace around it to cut out the stock. The material supplied in most plank-on-bulkhead kits for this purpose is not usually the right size, and in any case is not uniform throughout.

Use the back part of the jig as the pattern for the planked front part of the gunport lid. Remember when making the gunport lids that each gunport must match the square hole it is filling, both in the number of planks and their pattern. Many of the gunports run through the wales, and they must be included with the gunport lid. When the gunport lid is closed, it should blend right in with the existing planking as

if there was no lid there. Therefore, you cannot mass-produce gunport lids, but you must make each individually to fit into the existing run of the planking at its location. FIGURE 4-43 illustrates the right and wrong procedure.

Gratings

The gratings of a ship (FIG. 4-27) can ruin your model if not done correctly and to the right scale. This is one area of the plank-on-bulkhead ship model that is not properly supplied in the kits. Most of the kit models of this type that furnish grating material have the holes too large. If this size grating was used on the real ship, the crewman's foot would go through one of the holes.

Sometimes the kit will give you a hint or warning. An example is the model kit of the *Friesland* by Mamoli, which supplies much too large a set of gratings, but does show the proper size on the plans

Fig. 4-38. The stern of Dick Roos' H.M.S. Peregrine Galley.

Fig. 4-39. A close shot of my Elizabeth with the one lead scupper showing just below and between the two cannon.

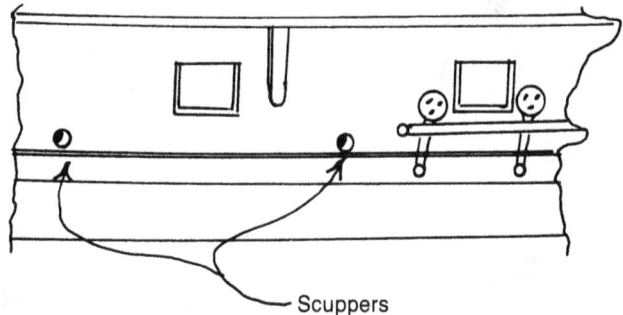

Fig. 4-40. A sketch of the scuppers as viewed from the outside of the hull.

Scuppers

of the ship. I used the plans of the ship to make my own set of gratings out of lemon wood for this ship and have gotten many comments and questions concerning them since they look so much better than some of the other kit-model gratings.

I made the gratings from a template. I spent much time trying to make gratings using several different methods. While doing this, I happened to walk into a hobby train shop with a friend one day and found

the perfect size grating, except that it was made out of plastic and not the right square shape. I purchased two of the plastic gratings and compared them to the plans of the *Friesland,* and they were a perfect fit. They became my templates, and I used them to make the gratings from some lemon wood, which I had cut to the right size. Using my Dremel drill and a drill press, I drilled the holes in the lemon wood, then used a small square file to very lightly square the holes,

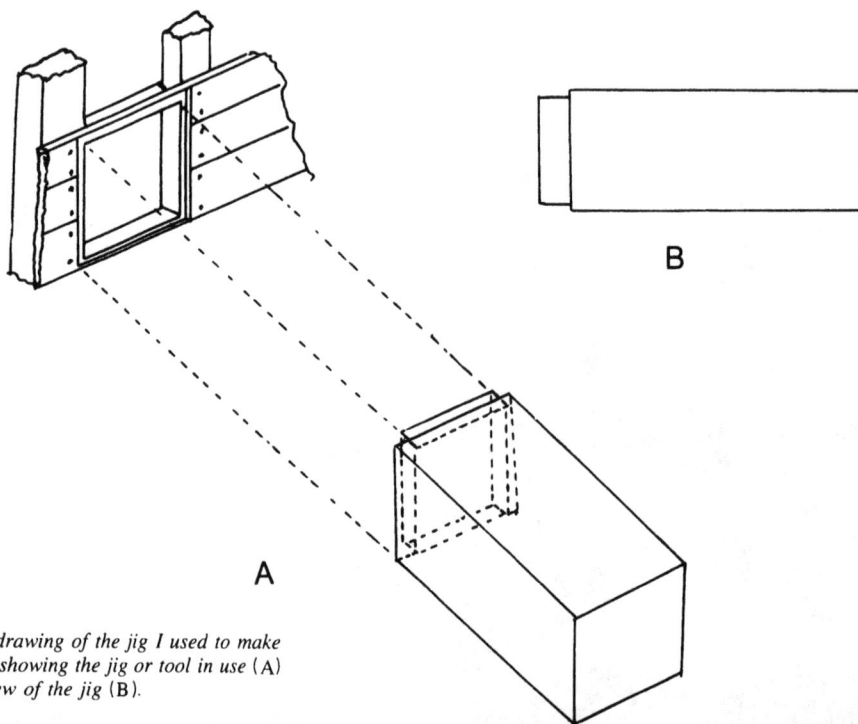

Fig. 4-41. A drawing of the jig I used to make the gunports, showing the jig or tool in use (A) and a side view of the jig (B).

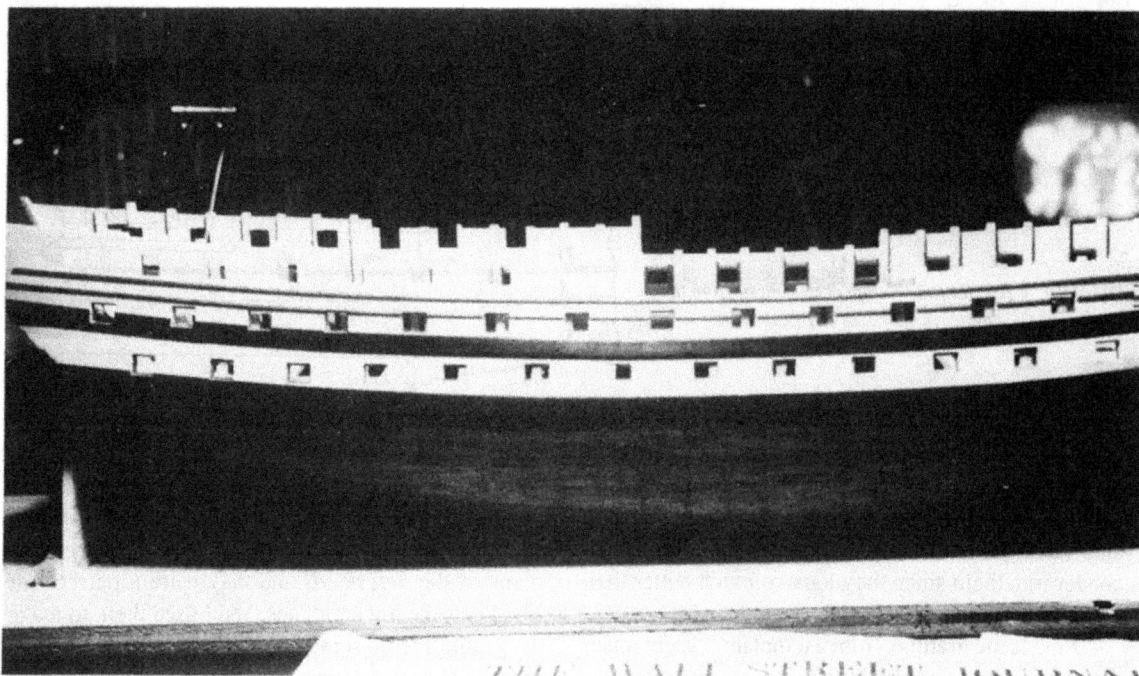

Fig. 4-42. Ed Marple's Conqueror showing the nice square gunports all of the same size. The jig drawn in Fig. 4-41 helps to achieve this accuracy. (Photo courtesy of Ed Marple.)

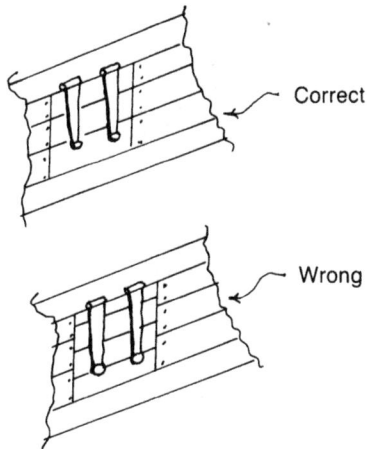

Fig. 4-43. *The right and wrong way to plank your gunports.*

although they are so small that it is hard to tell if they are round or not. (See FIG. 4-44).

This was my solution to the grating problem when I built the *Friesland*, but I would use a different method today. The books listed in the back of this text show many ways of making gratings, and you can take your pick.

Head Timbers

The bow of a vessel is a real problem for many beginning modelers, so I will spend a little time on the methods of making the difficult head timbers, which are not that hard if you work at it. This is another area that is very much lacking in the model ship kits, more so with the plank-on-bulkhead kits than

Fig. 4-44. *The gratings of the* Friesland *as described in the text. The commercial gratings supplied in the kit were very much out of scale, so this is one of the items you must remake if you want a scale job done.*

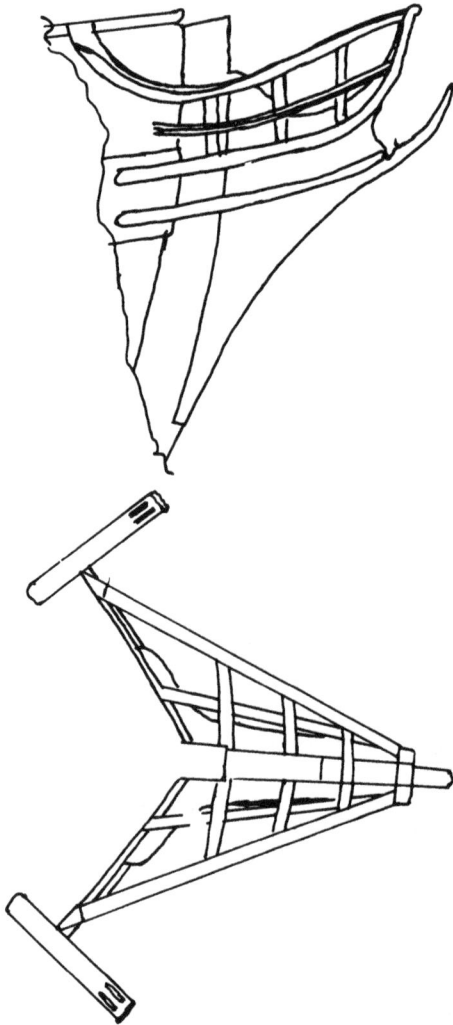

Fig. 4-45. A sketch of the two views of the head of a ship, which are required in order to do a good job of reproducing the head timbers.

with the solid-hull kits. The solid-hull kits at least give you a good plan to use.

Ideally you need a plan view of the head or a view looking down from above the head structure, and you need the side view and bow view or a view looking at the head from the side and from the front. I have found that trying to make a paper template of the head does not work. The only way to make the head timbers is to obtain a piece of wood in block form and carve or cut out the head timbers to get a pattern, and then transfer the final set of patterns of

all the head timbers to your good wood once you have made sure that everything fits as it should. FIGURE 4-45 illustrates a typical head set of plans of the *Fair American*, which was supplied with the Model Shipways solid-hull kit I built.

The most obvious part of the head is the *knee* of the head, which is the timber attached directly to the stem of your ship and is usually included as part of your stem in most kit models. The yacht *Mary* kit by Mamoli (FIG. 4-46) is an example of the simple head arrangement, with just the knee of the head and no head timbers. You do have decorations and cheeks on this stem, however, along with the unicorn figurehead.

You cannot treat this stem lightly, because it is the main support for the rest of your head work. It is the second most decorated part of your ship next to your stern, and can make a ship look really bad or good as the case may be. A poorly done head makes the rest of your model look shabby.

You can install the knee as part of the stem when you first set up your stem, keel, and sternpost structure, or you can add it after you have planked your ship. There are pros and cons for both methods. You want to get the knee of the head absolutely in line with the keel or your head will be crooked, which argues for installation in the beginning when it can be put under the glass with the rest of your keel structure. On the other hand, it is easier to plank with the knee of the head absent. Also, the knee of the head tends to get knocked off during construction. I have installed the knee of the head both before and after planking, with about the same results.

When installing the knee of the head, do not forget to add all of the details to the knee, such as the gammoning hole, holes for your tacks, and any other items that are best done now. After you have installed your head timbers, it will be very difficult to drill these holes. Tom Palen's model of the *Endeavour* shows the simplest form of the head with no knee at all but just the stem (FIG. 4-47).

The cheeks are the next item to install (FIG. 4-47). They are difficult to make. The best way I have found to tackle them is to obtain a piece of wood big enough to carve it to shape to fit the junction of the wales and the knee of the head. It will help to make a cardboard template first, then carve it out of wood, leaving a little bit of extra wood for final fitting. Take your time with this procedure. Make as good a fit as you can and avoid the use of wood filler. Do not despair if your first set does not fit right, but try again with a second set of cheeks.

Again, if all has been done correctly, you can use the port side as a guide for making the starboard side cheek, but the camber will be different. I think the cheeks are perhaps the most difficult timbers of the head to make.

Be sure to make your ship's *hawse holes* and *bolsters* at this time. The hawse holes are those holes in your hull from which the anchor rope comes through. The bolters are timbers just beneath the hawse holes (FIG. 4-48). If you have installed the lead scuppers for water drainage as discussed earlier in this text, you might also want to install lead lining in your hawse holes. The hawse holes should also be larger at their outer ends, or cambered. A simple hole drilled through the hull at the bow is not the way to do it. It only takes a few minutes to add this detail, and will separate your model from one that is almost as good.

The next step is to make the upper head rail. Look at the plan view or top view. You will see that the upper head rail is straight. I took a piece of wood, having the same thickness as the head rail from the ship's hull to the tip of the knee of the head, and the same depth as the highest point of the upper rail to its lowest point as shown on the elevation plan. I carbon-copied the views indicated in FIG. 4-49 onto the block of wood. Using my Dremel tool with sanding disks attached, I sanded away the excess wood of the block until I reached the shape of the upper head rail. I checked it many times with the hull to

Fig. 4-46. The model of my yacht Mary, *which shows the simple head structure of a small ship. Only the checks had to be done.*

Fig. 4-47. The even simpler head work of the H.M.S. Endeavour by Tom Palen under construction.

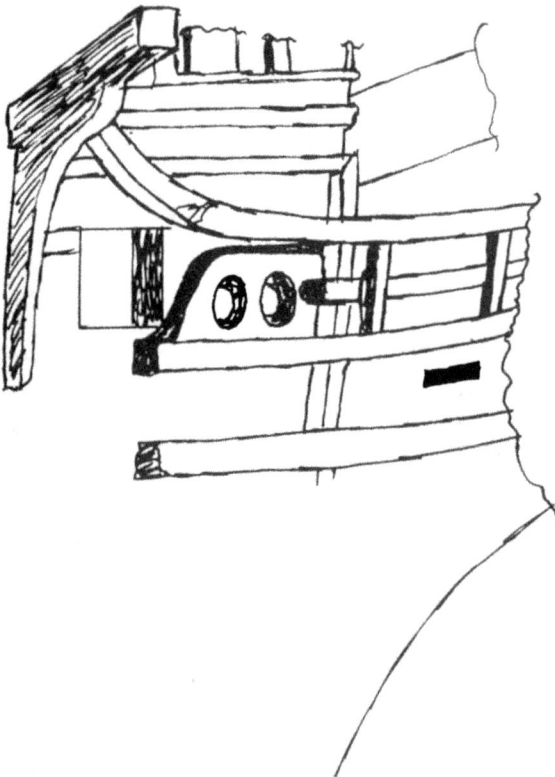

Fig. 4-48. A sketch showing the bolsters attached above the upper check into which the hawse holes are installed.

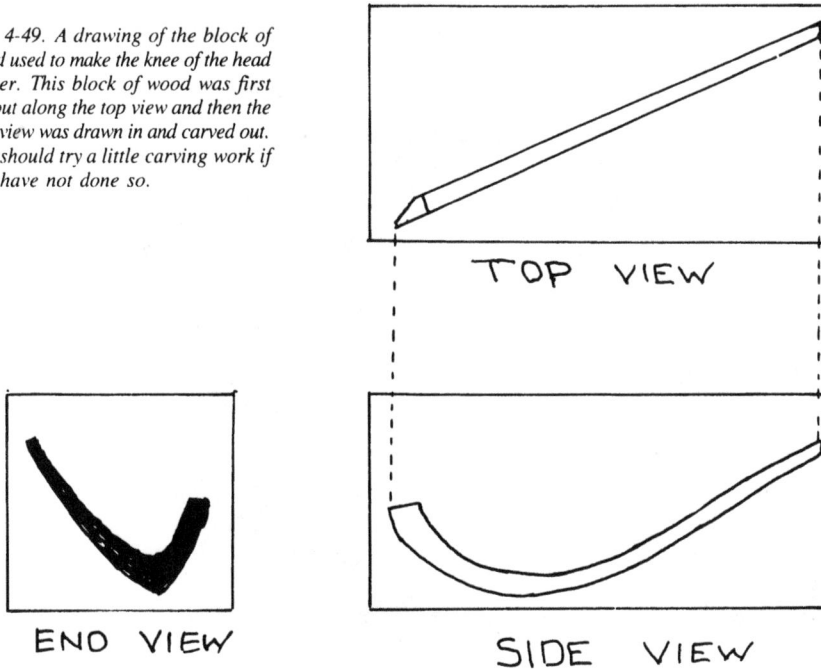

Fig. 4-49. A drawing of the block of wood used to make the knee of the head timber. This block of wood was first cut out along the top view and then the side view was drawn in and carved out. You should try a little carving work if you have not done so.

TOP VIEW

END VIEW

SIDE VIEW

make sure it would fit correctly, and I worked very slowly the closer I cam to the final shape. I had to make five of these to obtain the final two that fit.

I followed the same procedure with the lower head rail, although this one was not as difficult. I then made up the head timbers with the aid of the cardboard template. This is also a trial and error type of fitting. I threw away a number of the head timbers because they did not fit right.

The job is really not as difficult as it sounds and will leave you with a lot of satisfaction and pride when you have finished it. It is certainly a vast improvement over the head timbers furnished in most kit models. One known exception is the head timber provided with the Mamoli *Friesland* kit, which worked very well. With this kit, a flexible plywood piece was furnished, which when cut as described in the kit bent very nicely into the head rails. I still had to make the head timbers in the usual way. FIGURE 4-50 shows the *Friesland* kit model's head timber construction as completed on the model before the spritsail was installed.

Your head beams are the next things you must install. Two neat little items you can add are the seats of ease, which is one of the purposes of the ship's head. The beams are similar to deck beams and are fitted the same way as the deck beams, and gratings are also sometimes fitted (FIG. 4-51). For added detail, install lodging knees.

FIGURES 4-52 and 4-53 are fine examples of the completed head by several of the members of the S.M.A. The figures go from the rather simple type of head to the most complex headwork of the large warship.

There are many other details to complete before your ship is finished, but you have completed the main elements up to this point. The rails, deck houses, catheads, etc, should now be installed. You are not yet through with the planking process; you still must plank your ship's boat and the lower tops of your masts. These last items will be discusssed in Chapter 5.

Fig. 4-50. The head work of my model of the Friesland. *This is the first kit model I built that had a pretty good head layout, although the order in which the kit instructs you to do the work is not the best way of doing it and I did not follow it.*

Fig. 4-51. My Le Mirage *model, showing the grating installed at the head. Once again, the rigging is not done using the kit's instructions.*

Fig. 4-52. Dick Roos' model of H.M.S. Peregrine Galley, *showing his scratch efforts on the head timbers of a plank-on-bulkhead kit model.*

Fig. 4-53. A fine example of the head timbers and figurehead of a scratch-built ship of the line. This model is Ed Marple's H.M.S. Royal George. (Photo courtesy of Ed Marple.)

5

Planking A Ship's Boats

THE SHIP'S BOATS ARE ONE OF THE ITEMS THAT ARE not well done in kits but are also one of the items that will make your model ship excel if done right. I have seen many excellent ship models with either no ship's boats or ship's boats that did not come up to the excellent standard of the model ship on which they were installed. It is really not that difficult to make ship's boats, and the best and simplest way is to follow the methods of actual boat construction. FIGURES 5-1 and 5-2 show excellent examples of what ship's boats should look like.

WOODEN MOLD

The first step is to make a wooden mold of the inside of the ship's boat out of a block of wood. To make this mold use a wood that will hold its shape, and make sure the hull shape of the mold is slightly smaller than the final shape that is required. Add another piece of wood beneath the mold to act as a holder (FIG. 5-3). Mark on the mold the sheer line of your boat, as well as the keel line and your frame lines. Be sure to wax this mold heavily so that it does not stick to the frames when you remove it.

Cut out the stem, keel, and sternpost and notch them to receive the frames. Also, cut out a holder for the frames to hold the bottom of the frames in

place against the hull mold. This frame holder should be below the sheer line you made on your mold.

Soak small $\frac{1}{32}$-inch-square pieces of wood in household ammonia for about one hour. I have used the $\frac{1}{32}$-inch-square pieces of basswood available in hobby shops with excellent results. After soaking the wood in ammonia, remove and bend the frames over the wooden mold, inserting the ends of the wood into the notches cut in the holder (FIG. 5-4). Be sure to follow the line drawn on the mold, and check the position of each frame with the keel assembly being installed before you go on to the next frame. Once all of the frames are in place, put the keel assembly in place and let the entire unit sit for about 24 hours.

If everything still looks good, glue the keel assembly in position and proceed to plank the ship's boat much the same way you planked the ship's hull. Try to avoid getting any glue on the mold. Do not forget your stern piece.

Let the ship's boat dry for at least one day before you remove it from the mold. At this point, you can dowel the ship's boat planks using fine straws from a broom. The hull even at this point is strong.

Once the boat is removed from the mold, you can add the floor boards, gunwales, the thwarts, the gratings, and the other interior constructional details. FIGURE 5-5 shows the completed inside construction

Fig. 5-1. The boat on Henry Bridenbecker's model of the Irene. *Notice the detail added to the scratch-built boat.*

Fig. 5-2. A ship's boat on one of Ed Marple's models. Again, all of the detail in the boat, including the boat's oars, add a lot to the model. (Photo courtesy of Ed Marple.)

Fig. 5-3. The molds used by Bob Saddoris to make his boats. The small mold in the front is for an addition to a model, and the larger mold in the back is for a large model of a dinghy.

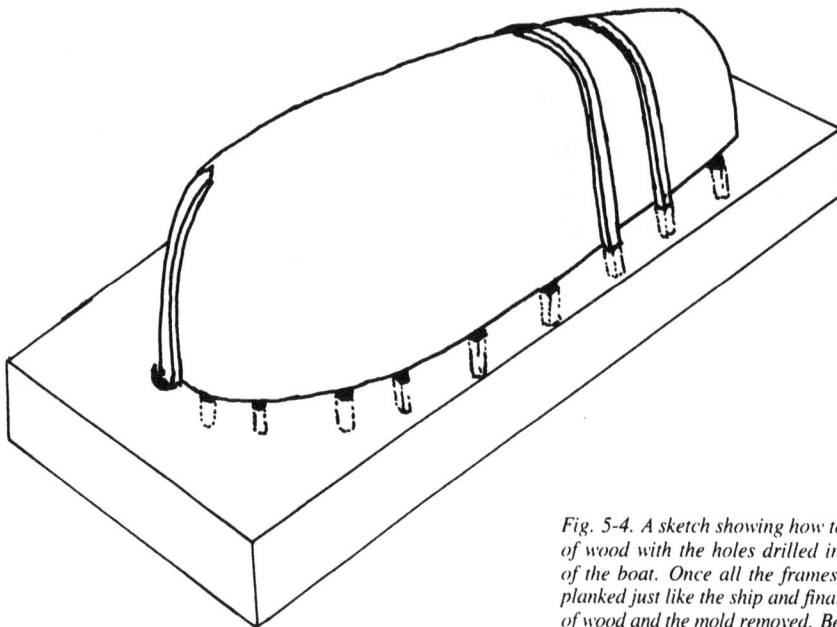

Fig. 5-4. A sketch showing how to use the mold and a block of wood with the holes drilled into it to accept the frames of the boat. Once all the frames are installed, the boat is planked just like the ship and finally cut away from the block of wood and the mold removed. Be sure to wax the mold good so you can remove it after planking your boat.

of a whaleboat and also shows what details can be added to the boat to improve its appearance.

USING THE KIT BOATS

You can use the ship's boats supplied in the kits if you wish, since you did pay for them. Take the supplied hull of the ship's boat and throw everything else away. Use a Dremel or similar tool to hollow out the ship's hull itself until the boat is very thin. You can check to see how thin it is by holding it up to a strong light. If you can see through it, you are pretty close.

Once your boat is thinned out enough, draw lines to guide you with the positioning of the frames. Then add the ribs to the boat by soaking them in ammonia and then bending them into the boat. Then lay your keelson, floor boards, etc., much like in FIG. 5-5. FIGURE 5-6 shows a *Grand Banks* dory under construction with some of the inside details being installed. An interesting item on this model is the hull fastenings, which are of annealed iron wire and copper wire to simulate the actual rivets used.

PLANKING USING THE CLINKER METHOD

If your kit model has a plastic ship's boat, you can make your own, which will look better than the plastic ship's boat. You can construct the boat at any time during the building of your ship model. Some modelers have even gone to the extent of building the ship's boat first before they begin building the ship model. Other modelers have built large models of ship's boats as a project in itself, and there are some kits available of large-scale ship's boats, which are plank-on-frame and are built over a mold.

There are also two different types of planking for the ship's boats—carvel and clinker—as described earlier. All of the commercially available kits are carvel-type construction, so to build the clinker type of boat you will have to go scratch. You can try your hand at building a Viking ship, which is clinker built, and there are some manufacturers that make this type of kit. The scratch-built model of the *Grand Banks* dory shown in FIG. 5-6 is another boat that is clinker built.

The rules for the clinker or lapstrake type of

construction given at the end of Chapter 3 apply to clinker boat construction, as well as ship construction. I will go through the method of planking this type of boat for modeling purposes. You first need good boat plans, if obtainable. Underhill makes an excellent set of boat plans, and I am sure others are available. I have yet to see any boat plans included with a model ship kit.

Using the boat plans, your first step is to make a mold of the boat to the inside of the planking. The pictures of Bob Saddoris' lapstrake boat and the mold he used to make it with are shown in FIG. 5 7 Bob made the mold by taking four frames from the plan of the boat and filling in the spaces with a hard balsa wood. Bob says the hard balsa wood he used worked fine to hold the shape of his boat while he planked the hull.

The next step is to make the stern, keel, and sternpost structure. Cut the rabbet carefully into the keel structure to receive the planks. Then wax the mold well to prevent the completed boat from sticking to the mold when you are done. Then plank the boat in the clinker type style.

You will need to calculate the thickness of your planks in order to cover the hull area of the boat, much the same way as you did your ship. You also will need to make the planks wider than ordinary to account for the width in the overlap of the planks. Mark the frame positions on the mold before you start to plank, but unlike the carvel method, you will plank the boat first, and add the ribs later. This method might seem strange, but it is the way they really did this type of construction and still do today. The builders of the real thing today even use the same mold to make dozens of the same boat.

When planking the boat, make sure the *sheer strake,* or the plank just below the boat rail, is a little wider by the width of the rail (FIG. 5-8). The first plank to be installed is the garboard strake, and you can install it much the same way you did for the ship model. Then install the second and subsequent planks (FIG. 5-8). The planks will taper as they do in the real ship, and you should again have just as many planks at the bow area as you do amidships. There is additional taper because the planks will overlap midship, but will slowly become less of an overlap

Fig. 5-5. Another type of boat model which is a model in itself. This is a fine example of a kit boat model of a whale boat by Pan Art. The model was built by Jack Wilson.

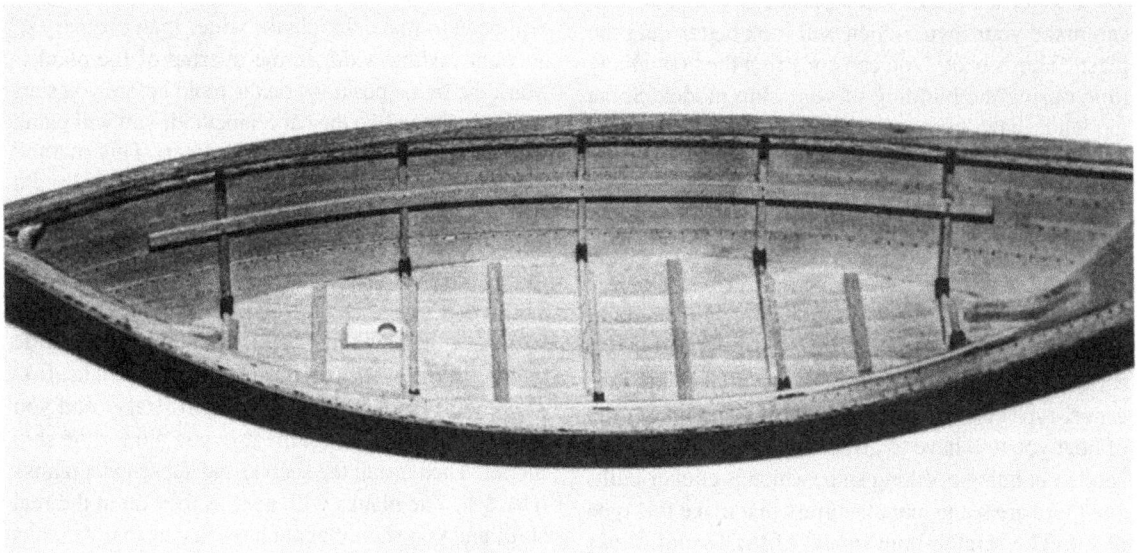

Fig. 5-6. A boat by Dave Yotter of a Grand Banks dory, which is scratch. This boat is under construction and gives a good example of the internal details you can put into a boat.

as you go to the stern. The bow and will eventually become carvel type planking when the planks enter the rabbet at either end.

Once the planking has been completed, leave the model for a period to let the glue dry, then remove it from the mold. You will now need to add the ribs and all of the other internal details of your boat to complete it, much the same as the other ship's boats detailed previously. Dowel (it might be more correct to use clinch nails or rivets) the finished planking after you install the ribs or frames. If you have the plans with the details, you should also add whatever details you can to your boat.

The outer planking of Bob Saddoris' model of his dinghy with the frames installed after the planking has been completed is shown in FIG. 5-9. The dinghy planking that Bob has done is so thin that you can easily see light through the planks.

PLANKING ON THE MASTS

The last items you will plank on your ship model will be done while you are involved in the masting and rigging of your ship model. This step involves planking the tops on your fore, main, and mizzen masts (FIG. 5-10). The best procedure in planking the tops is to follow the same practice as the real builders of these ships, shown in FIG. 5-11.

This is the final bit of planking that you will do on your ship model. If you have followed the outlines in this book or have modified the procedures to suit your own needs with the same results, you can be

Fig. 5-7. Bob Saddoris' mold, along with the boat that was made from it in the background.

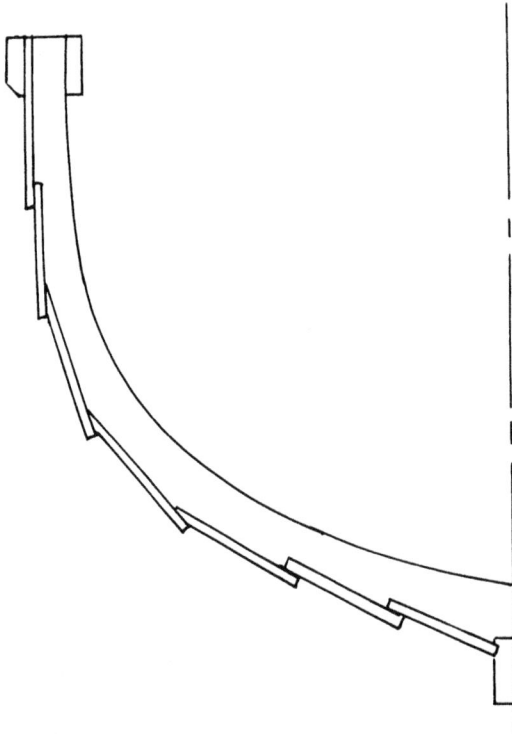

Fig. 5-8. Clinker-type construction of a ship's boat as used by Bob Saddoris when he built the dinghy shown in Fig. 5-9.

Fig. 5-9. The outside of Bob's dinghy, showing the clinker type of construction. The planks are so thin in some places that you can see daylight through them if you hold the boat up to the light.

Fig. 5-10. The main top of my Friesland which is fully planked and detailed. The kit-provided top was used for a pattern to cut the round outside of the top.

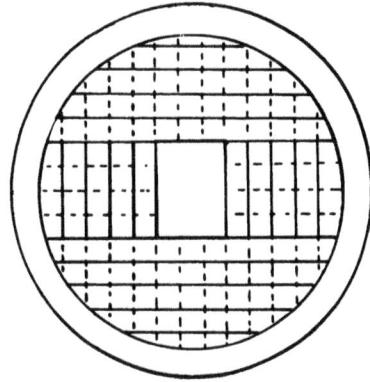

Fig. 5-11. A sketch of the planking of a typical top. The shape of the top varied. In essence, you have two layers of planks laid one over the other.

proud of your achievement. You will also know that you have built the model much like the real thing. The main point to remember is to take your time and to not be satisfied with second best. FIGURES 5-12 through 5-17 show some fine examples of both kit and scratch models that have been built following the basic procedures outlined in this text. Each modeler has his own techniques and no two are the same, so do not be afraid to modify and invent new ways to plank your model, as long as you get basically the same result.

You should be able to leave your model in your work area throughout the entire period of building, which can mean more than one year in many cases. This is not a necessity, but is strongly recommended, and is the final requirement to successfully planking your model and getting the maximum enjoyment from the process.

So as to not leave you at the stage of completing your planking and not knowing where to go next to complete your model, I have included a complete list of all the books I have on masting and rigging a ship model. To my knowledge, there is no plank-on-bulkhead kit that has a complete and accurate masting, rigging, and sail plan included with the instructions.

Fig. 5-12. A photo of the Scottish Maid *by Joe Seela. This is a scratch-built model which was painted. Notice the frames visible where the planks have been left off.*

Fig. 5-13. The Rattlesnake *by Alan Ikemura as completed. This is an excellent example of a kit model.*

Fig. 5-14. The Peregrine Galley *by Dick Roos as completed. This is an excellent example of what can be done with a kit model that is extensively modified. Dick consulted other plans and used his own wood.*

Fig. 5-15. The final appearance of the H.M.S. Conqueror *by Ed Marple.* (Photo courtesy of Ed Marple.)

Fig. 5-16. The beautiful Egyptian ship by Bob Saddoris. The detail on this model is a real craftsman's delight.

Fig. 5-17. A fine example of a plank-on-bulkhead kit model of the Dutch gun boat by Mantua as built by Dick Roos.

132

A

U.S. Maritime Museums

Atwater Kent Museum	Philadelphia, PA
Boston Marine Museum	Boston, MA
Chesapeake Bay Maritime Museum	St. Michaels, MD
Francis Russel Hart Nautical Museum	Cambridge, MA
Great Lakes Museum	Detroit, MI
Marine Museum of the City of New York	New York, NY
Mariners Museum	Newport News, VA
Museum of Science and Industry	Chicago, IL
Mystic Seaport	Mystic, CT
Naval Historical Foundation	Washington, DC
Peabody Museum of Salem	Salem, MA
Penobscot Marine Museum	Searsport, ME
Philadelphia Maritime Museum	Philadelphia, PA
Portsmouth Naval Shipyard Museum	Portsmouth, VA
The River Museum	Marietta, OH
San Francisco Maritime Museum	San Francisco, CA
Smithsonian Institution	Washington, DC
Star of India	San Diego, CA
U.S. Naval Academy	Annapolis, MD

B

European Maritime Museums

Altonaer Museum	Hamburg, W. Germany
Imperial War Museum	London, England
Marinmuseum och Modelkammaren	Karlskrona, Sweden
Maritiem Museum "Prins Hendrik"	Rotterdam, Netherlands
Musee de la Marine	Paris, France
Musee de la Marine	Rochefort, France
Museo Storico Navale	Venice, Italy
Museo Naval	Madrid, Spain
Museo Maritimo	Barcelona, Spain
National Maritime Museum	Greenwich, England
Nationaal Scheepvaart Museum	Antwerp, Belgium
Naval Museum of Greece	Athen-piraus, Greece
Nederlandsch Historisch Scheepvaart Museum	Amsterdam, Netherlands
Norsk Sjofartsmuseum	Oslo, Norway
Orlogsmuseet	Copenhagen, Denmark
Sandefjord Sjofartsmuseum	Sandefjord, Norway
Science Museum South Kensington	London, England
Statens Sjohistoriska Museum	Stockholm, Sweden
Vikingskiphuset	Oslo, Norway

6

References for Rigging

The Anatomy of Nelson's Ships by C. Nepean Longridge
The Baltimore Clipper by Howard Irving Chapelle
Historic Ship Models by Wolfram zu Mondfled
The Masting and Rigging of English Ships of War 1625-1860 by James Lees
Plank-on-Frame Models and Scale Masting and Rigging Volume II by Harold A. Underhill (Glasgow, 1958)
Rees's Naval Architecture (1819-20) by Abraham Rees
The Rigging of Ships in the Days of the Spritsail Topmast 1600-1720 by R. C. Anderson
Steel's Elements of Mastmaking, Sailmaking and Rigging arranged, with an introduction by Claude S. Gill
Ship Model Builder's Assistant by Charles G. Davis (New York, 1970)

Index

Edited by Suzanne L. Cheatle